SOUL
or the
SPIRIT

*Knowing the difference
can change your life*

—RAPHAEL GIGLIO—

DEDICATION

This book is dedicated to my wife Aly, who not only encouraged and assisted me in the writing of it, but helps me try to live it out every day of our life together. Also, to my daughters Phoebe and Abigail for being my constant inspiration. And to my church North Shore Fellowship, you have all given me the freedom and opportunity to speak and write the things that the Lord has laid upon my heart for you, and for whomever has ears to hear.

Author's Note: Several of the terms that are used in this book do not have identical standard definitions among various theologians and biblical scholars. Some of the basic words such as *Body, Soul, Spirit, Heart, Flesh, Mind, Emotions, and Will* may have slightly different definitions in other biblical applications or contexts in which they are found. Some will have varying meanings between New Testament and Old Testament texts and even between separate usages of the words from the same writer in different passages. I have tried to remain consistent and true to the intended meaning of each of the words and phrases as they appear in the scriptures selected for this topic. I believe that you'll find a high level of consistency and accuracy in the contextual meaning of these words as they are used in each of the biblical texts that are presented. I've specifically given very careful attention and consideration to the biblical definitions of the words *Body, Soul, Spirit, Heart*, and *Flesh*, and how they apply in these contexts.

You will notice that a lower-case "s" is used in the word *spirit* when referring to the human spirit or any other spirit. When referring to a person's regenerated spirit or the Holy Spirit however, a capital "S" is used.

I am also aware that several of the perspectives brought forth in this study have a variety of different viewpoints, as is the case with most theological topics. For instance, many well-respected and scholarly individuals hold a dichotomist view of man and may disagree with some of what is presented in this book. I only ask that we would all continually seek God humbly and earnestly for however much of the *depths of the riches of His wisdom and knowledge* He would care to graciously bestow upon us as feeble, flawed, but faithful students of His Word.

"O the depth of the riches both of the wisdom and knowledge of God! How unsearchable are his judgments, and his ways past finding out!"(Romans 11:33 KJV)

CONTENTS

FOREWORD

You've just watched the news and are now feeling a heavy burden of worry about the economy, an emerging health crisis, rampant immorality, or the growing tension in world affairs.

You've just spent a few minutes on social media and now find yourself angry at someone or something or disgusted with aspects of society that you find disturbing or alarming.

You've just spoken to a friend, a family member, or your doctor and were told something that induces so much fear, anxiety, sadness, or stress in you that it grips your mind and emotions in such a way that you find it difficult to find relief.

You know that the Bible tells us, "Don't worry" and "Give thanks in all things." You've also read that Christians are supposed to have an abundance of "love," "joy," and "perfect peace" in all things, but you don't feel any of that now. In fact, in some ways, you feel the opposite.

Why?

The key to finding the answer to this is in understanding the difference between the soul and the spirit.

Let's face it, the times we are living in are often difficult, troublesome, and unsettling. Many of us fall prey to the tendency to worry, get angry, or become afraid. This can often lead to discouragement, anxiety, and even depression. We read the news, we hear the stories, we feel conflict and distress, and we see endless unrest and trouble throughout the world.

It is natural to be very concerned. Everything we *sense* compels us to be alarmed and uneasy about things taking place all around us. We can't help but internalize it, and before long we find ourselves disenchanted or hopeless instead of faith-filled and joyful.

It's a constant battle within us.

In one sense, we trust God and know that He is Lord over everything on the earth, and in the spirit realm as well.

In another sense, we are troubled and concerned about the darkness we live in and among, and we often become disturbed by it.

We feel it all around us and within us. Sometimes in overwhelming waves of thoughts and emotions that are more than we can bear.

That is because there's a battle going on *all around* us. There is also a battle going on *within* each one of us.

The battle within us is between two opposing forces: the flesh and the spirit. Our *flesh* wants to please and satiate the desires of the body, while our *spirit* was created to commune with God's Spirit within us. This conflict is played out in the battleground of "the soul."

The key to winning this battle, and enjoying life and peace even in the most difficult times, is understanding the *difference* between the soul and the spirit. Sadly, when these two terms are confused and conflated, we end up relying on mental and emotional resources in situations that require spiritual wisdom and strength.

My hope is that this book will help us clearly see *the difference between the soul and the spirit.*

Once we can identify the unique characteristics of each one, we will find it much easier to walk by the Spirit and live in the beauty and blessing of the fruit of the Spirit, in both our relationship with God and our relationships with others.

> "The mind governed by the flesh is death, but the mind governed by the Spirit is life and peace." (Romans 8:6 NIV)

INTRODUCTION

SOUL OR THE SPIRIT

Do you know the difference between your soul and your spirit?

How about the difference between your heart or your flesh?

Many people can't clearly describe these things, let alone find Bible verses that clearly explain them, but having a clear understanding of them is key to having lasting peace and an abundant life.

Scripture tells us that we are each made up of three parts: body, soul, and spirit.

> "May God himself, the God of peace, sanctify you through and through. May your whole *spirit, soul,* and *body* be kept blameless at the coming of our Lord Jesus Christ" (1st Thessalonians 5:23 NIV)

In this book, we will look carefully at each of these three parts to see what they are and how God created them to function.

The body is easiest to identify—it's simply our physical anatomy.

The soul and the spirit, however, are a little more difficult to understand because they are immaterial. We need help from the Word of God.

> "For the word of God is alive and active. Sharper than any double-edged sword, it penetrates even to dividing soul and spirit." (Hebrews 4:12a NIV)

Have you ever read this particular scripture and wondered what the writer was specifically talking about, or about the deeper meaning behind it?

It's very important that we understand the difference between the soul and the spirit. Without this understanding, we are at risk of experiencing constant stress, discouragement, unfulfillment, and confusion as we try to navigate through life, instead of the perfect peace, lasting joy, and abundant life that God intends for us.

CHAPTER 1

DIVIDING THE SOUL AND SPIRIT

"For the word of God is alive and active. Sharper than any double-edged sword, it penetrates even to dividing soul and spirit,"
(Hebrews 4:12a NIV)

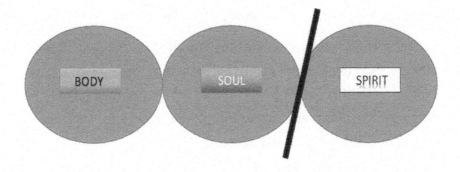

Do you understand the difference between your soul and the spirit?

What do you think of when you hear the phrase *"dividing soul and spirit"*?

As we look into what the Word of God has to say about these things, and study some very familiar scriptures, I want to challenge you to read with a new understanding and fresh perspective. Some of the verses will be those that you have heard many times but have never fully understood. Others will be those you've read for many years but have just never thought about in this context before.

I encourage you to be open to listening to what the Spirit is saying to you in this season of your life as you study this topic. My hope is that you will draw new inspiration out of old scriptures, beginning with a word *from* the Word *about* "the Word."

> "For the word of God is alive and active. Sharper than any double-edged sword, it penetrates even to *dividing soul* and *spirit*." (Hebrews 4:12a NIV)

You may have read this verse many times before, but did you ever stop to ask what "dividing *soul* and *spirit*" really means? Aren't the soul and the spirit one and the same, and if so, why would the Word of God want to divide them?'

The truth is that they are *not* the same; the Word of God "divides" them by showing us distinctions between the two in scripture. The soul is very different from the spirit. Each functions in entirely different ways. Both are important in their own right, and neither should be diminished or disregarded.

Our soul (mind and emotions) can sometimes lead us to thoughts, actions, behaviors, or opinions that seem reasonable in the natural but are contrary to what the Spirit is saying to us through the Word of God. It is of great importance that we allow the Word of God to divide our soul and spirit and help us to know the difference between the two. It could be confusing at times, discerning between the soul's responses and the Spirit's leading. We may experience certain strong thoughts and feelings that we attribute to spiritual impulses, but which could very well be soulish reactions that are actually contrary to the Spirit. The Word of God gives us clarity on these things. Important truths in the Bible are constantly made alive to us by the Spirit and compel us to think differently and act contrary to the tendencies of our human nature. This is why it is so important to study and know the Word of God in order to be able to rightly divide the soul and spirit.

The living, powerful Word of God helps us to know the difference between these two very important aspects of our being in real time because it is living and active. One of the main reasons we need to know the difference between the two is that they are at war with each other. One has the potential of pleasing God and drawing our whole being toward Him, and the other tends to want to please itself and draw us away from intimacy with God.

> The SOUL: The soul is simply our *mind and emotions.*
> What we *think* and what we *feel, which* can also
> determine our *will.* It could be said that our soul is
> our Mind, Emotions, and in effect our Will.

> The SPIRIT: The part of us that is regenerated by
> God's Spirit. It is that part that enables us to connect
> and commune with God.

SOUL

Our soul is comprised of *our mind* and *our emotions* and forms *our will.* Our *will* plays an extremely important role in our lives.

It can direct us to either choose to submit to God and experience the many blessings of God OR reject God and experience severe consequences as a result. The outcome of this choice can be as minimal as missing out on little blessings from God throughout the day, or as consequential as the difference between eternal life or eternal damnation.

Our soul is by its fallen nature inclined to please the *flesh*, but when we are made alive in the Spirit, our soul can be directed to please God by trusting in Him "with all our *heart*" (Proverbs 3:5). It's a constant battle, an internal tug-of-war that takes place between the soul (represented by the flesh) and the spirit, which along with the heart has been made new.

> "I will give you a new heart and put a new spirit in you." (Ezekiel 36:26a NIV)

SPIRIT

The spirit is the internal, immaterial, nonphysical, and non-psychological part of our being, capable of communing with God and others in a spiritual capacity. There are two spirits that we must understand: our human spirit and the Holy Spirit of God.

> "The Spirit himself testifies with our spirit that we are God's children" (Romans 8:16 NIV).

We begin with our human spirit. This is that part of us that was created with the capacity to receive and be made alive through the Holy Spirit. God's intention is that we receive His Spirit and the two are made one, much like air filling up a deflated balloon.

"But whoever is united with the Lord is one with him in spirit." (1st Corinthians 6:17 NIV)

DIVIDING SOUL AND SPIRIT

The Word of God is the guide in dividing the soul and the spirit. It is living and powerful so it helps us to clearly see what is the *soul* and what is the *spirit*.

It is so important to understand the difference so that we can be led into the truth by God's Spirit, instead of being held captive by our own thoughts and emotions.

Verses like 1st Corinthians 2:14 are clear examples of how the Word of God divides between the soul and the spirit. They show the stark difference between the natural man—he who operates exclusively in the soul realm—and the spiritual man—he who has been made alive in the Spirit and can receive and discern the things of the Spirit.

> "But the natural man does not receive the things of the Spirit of God, for they are foolishness to him; nor can he know *them,* because they are spiritually discerned." (1st Corinthians 2:14 NKJV)

The natural man is equipped only with his mind and emotions (soul). He is what A. B. Simpson calls the *psychical man.*

> *In I Cor. 2, the apostle Paul very clearly distinguishes between the soul and the spirit in man. The psychical man, that is, the soul man, he tells us, "receiveth not the things of the Spirit of God neither can he know them for they are spiritually discerned, but he that*

is spiritual discerneth all things." The psychical man, therefore, is the man of the soul, the spiritual man is the man of quickened spirit. It will be noticed that in this passage he begins with the spirit and gradually descends to the soul and body as the subjects of sanctification. This is quite instructive and significant. (A. B. Simpson)[1]

As we look deeper into the scriptures on this subject, we find that the soul and the spirit are not only different from each other but are also in conflict with each other. This conflict is why we feel so much stress and tension not only in the world but even within our own selves. The flesh, which is part of our soul, desires one thing, and the Spirit desires the complete opposite.

"For the *flesh* desires what is contrary to the *Spirit*, and the *Spirit* what is contrary to the *flesh*. *They are in conflict with each other*". (Galatians 5:17a NIV)

And to make matters worse, the world we live in is a war zone, complete with mental and emotional land mines, hidden traps, and enemy artillery. Many of the things we see, hear, read, and experience in the world have all been hijacked by the enemy whose intention is to keep us bound to and focused on the soul (mind/emotions) and *not* the Spirit.

"The mind governed by the flesh is death, but the mind governed by the Spirit is life and peace." (Romans 8:6 NIV)

Remember, it's a real battle, with a real enemy. Our enemy, the devil, wants to influence our soul (mind/emotions/will) to pull against God and the things of the Spirit. He wants to influence our soul to react to this battle by thinking, feeling, and decision-making under the direction of the flesh, rather than having our mind (soul) controlled by the Spirit through our heart.

Most of this battle takes place within our mind and emotions, in other words in what *we think* and in what *we feel*. That is the enemy's most strategic method of influencing our will. Every day we find ourselves constantly bombarded with provocative media, incendiary information, misleading communications, hostile exchanges, intentional deceptions, and fear-inducing information that is designed to discourage, frustrate, or even confuse us.

We become overwhelmed with such an enormous amount of stressful thoughts and inflammatory emotions that are stirred up by what we think and feel, that we often find ourselves, anxious, frustrated, annoyed, angry, and sometimes even gripped with fear. That is the goal of the enemy. He wants to keep us "walking in the soul." He wants us to be completely driven and controlled by our minds and emotions instead of by God's Spirit.

The Bible tells us, however, to *"walk in the Spirit"* (Gal. 5:16), and explains what it looks like when we do:

> "But the fruit of the Spirit is love, joy, peace, longsuffering, kindness, goodness, faithfulness, gentleness, self-control." (Galatians 5:22–23a NKJV)

How can we have peace, joy, patience, or even self-control when we are in the middle of so much crisis, tension, and dissonance? What does it actually mean to "walk in the Spirit"? The answers to these questions and all questions are found in the Word of God.

The Lord wants us to have victory in this battle and wants us to live a life of peace. Do you want to experience this victory every day and do away with the stress, anxiety, fear, and anger that try to invade your life through your soul? He has given us all that we need to overcome the daily attacks of the enemy, but we must understand the difference between the soul and the spirit to do so.

In the following chapters, we will explore what it means to walk in the Spirit, compared to what it means to walk in the soul, using verses from several books in the Bible. We will often refer to several key scriptures about the *body, soul,* and *spirit.* We will also look at the ones that mention the "Heart" and the "Flesh," and we will see the role that these two play in connection with the body, soul, and spirit.

My hope is that you will come away with a deeper understanding of who you are, body, soul, and spirit, and learn to better experience God's joy, peace, strength, and comfort in all three.

CHAPTER 2

BODY, SOUL, AND SPIRIT

"May your whole *spirit*, *soul* and *body* be kept blameless at
the coming of our Lord Jesus Christ"
(1st Thessalonians 5:23b NIV)

To fully understand the difference between the soul and the spirit, we need to understand the entire makeup of who we are and how we are created. That includes not just the soul and spirit, but the body as well. The term used to describe an entity made up of three unique parts is "Tripartite."

The Word of God reveals to us that we are made up of three primary parts: body, soul, and spirit, which make us *trichotomous* (having three parts). This concept, which is sometimes referred to as *trichotomy*, is supported throughout the Bible in various verses. The key verse for our study is 1st Thessalonians 5:23. It is here where we see most clearly that we are comprised of these three unique parts.

"May God himself, the God of peace, sanctify you through and through. May your whole spirit, soul, and body be kept blameless at the coming of our Lord Jesus Christ." (1st Thessalonians 5:23 NIV)

Paul tells us that these three parts are how he identifies a whole person, whom he prays that God would "sanctify through and through." He carefully identifies each of these and is careful to use the words that describe them best.

1. Spirit (Greek: *pneuma*)

2. Soul (Greek: *psuchē*)

3. Body (Greek: *sōma*)

Pastor Chuck Smith compared our trichotomy to the concept of the tripart divine Trinity. We, as those made in His image also function as three-in-one; however, in our case, we exist as an "inferior trinity"—our spirit is the part that communes with God.

"The *superior* Trinity is made up of the Father, Son, and Holy Spirit.

The *inferior* trinity is the spirit, soul, and body of man. And it is in the realm of the spirit where man meets God." (Pastor Chuck Smith)[2]

Each of us is intentionally designed by our Creator with these three unique parts of our being. Each is different, but each is necessary. Each gives us the ability to relate to God and others in unique ways.

Charles Spurgeon presents trichotomy with an emphasis on the spirit as the power of the three.

"Man consists of three parts, body, soul, and spirit, and the spirit is the power of the three." (C. H. Spurgeon)[3]

Watchman Nee, whose powerful ministry transformed Christian culture in China nearly one hundred years ago through preaching, church-planting, and theological works, writes very clearly on this subject:

"The Bible never confuses spirit and soul as though they are the same. Not only are they different in terms; their very natures differ from each other. The Word of God does not divide man into the two parts of soul and body. It treats man, rather, as "tripartite," spirit, soul, and body." (Watchman Nee)[4]

There have been several forms of diagrams that have emerged in the study of trichotomy, or body, soul, and spirit. Probably the most popular version is the concentric version created by Watchman Nee as a diagram in his book *The Release of the Spirit*.

Nee places the spirit at the center of the concentric diagram, emphasizing it as the innermost entity, and the body as the most external, with the soul in between. He even compares it with the structure of the Temple, with the outer court being the most common area, the Holy Place as the area by which one can draw close to God, and of course the Holy of Holies at the center, the dwelling place of God. This is an excellent analogy, especially since Paul describes our spirit as our "inner man." His diagram is accurate and effective in this context; however, for our purposes, we will most often refer to the lateral diagram (below) that I have created to compare and show the dynamics of the relationship between the three parts.

This diagram allows us to look at each part separately within the whole of one individual. We will study each part specifically, using scripture to see how they relate to one another. We will also look at other components within them, particularly parts of the soul.

So, now having identified the three parts of our tripart being, let's look at each one and see what it is and what it does.

BODY, SOUL, AND SPIRIT

BODY – (easiest to identify)

This is our physical body, our temporary "tent" that we are housed in while here on earth. It is designed by God with senses, behaviors, and survival instincts.

SOUL – (a little more difficult to describe)

This is our internal self. Our *minds* and our *emotions*, both of which form our *will*.

SPIRIT – (who we are *spiritually*)

This is the spiritual part of us that is made alive when we are saved. It is the part of us that God indwells and empowers by His Spirit. "*It is in the realm of the spirit where man meets God.*"

All three parts of our being are unique and important. Each functions separately but alongside the other parts to make us who we are physically, mentally, emotionally, and spiritually.

THE SOUL OR THE SPIRIT?

It's very common for people to confuse their soul and their spirit since these two invisible aspects of our being are not quite as easily identifiable as our bodies are. That's why we need the Word of God to "divide," or *help make a distinction* between the two. A. W. Tozer confesses that he sometimes got confused between "*soulish*" expressions and "*spiritual*" worship.

"It seems, Lord, that I sometimes become caught up in soulish expressions of worship and mistake them for

spiritual worship - my spirit communing with Your Spirit." (A.W. Tozer)[5]

It will help us all to think about the spiritual part of our being the way Tozer did. The part of us that goes beyond our thoughts and feelings. The part of us that is deeper than that which our mind and emotions could fully grasp. The spiritual part of us, where God's Spirit *communes* with our spirit.

"The Spirit himself testifies with our spirit that we are God's children." (Romans 8:16 NIV)

So now, let's take a closer look at the key verse that helps us understand the difference between the soul and the spirit:

"For the word of God *is* living and powerful, and sharper than any two-edged sword, piercing even to the division of *soul and spirit*, and of *joints* and *marrow* and is a discerner of the *thoughts and intents* of the *heart."* (Hebrews 4:12 NKJV)

This is the primary verse where we find the words *soul* and *spirit* mentioned together in the same sentence. This is where we begin to understand the difference between the two and the fact that the Word of God helps us divide them. It seems at first glance, however, as though the author of Hebrews is suggesting that we are made up of not just two or three parts, but lists seven unique aspects, and the Word of God is able to divide and discern between all of them. Does that mean we are made up of all these, instead of just the three we talked about? What do all these terms mean, and what part of "us" are they?

As we study this closer, we see that each of the aspects listed in addition to soul and spirit are components or subcomponents of these two, or are parts of the body.

SOUL – The internal part of us that is made up of our mind and emotions. These often determine our will.

SPIRIT – The part that is made alive (regenerated) at rebirth and "communes with God"

JOINTS – Part of the BODY. Referring to the bones and frame.

MARROW – Part of the BODY. Referring to the intricate workings of our physical design.

THOUGHTS – Part of the SOUL. Our minds and ideas.

INTENTS – Part of the SOUL. Our will and intentions.

> HEART – Part of the SOUL. Our deepest emotions, feelings, and innermost passions. Usually, it determines our will.

While we mostly focus on aspects of the soul and spirit in this study, it is important to mention the body as well, especially in light of Hebrews 4:12. The author writes that the Word of God is effective in not only "piercing to the division of" the *soul and spirit*, but also the *joints* and *marrow* (parts of the body) as well. The phrase "piercing to the division of" obviously does not mean surgically dissecting the bones and marrow of a human body, but it is more closely related to the phrase "rightly dividing," which Paul uses in 2nd Timothy 2:15 when he encourages Timothy to be faithful in "*rightly dividing the word of truth.*"

The Word of God, when correctly applied in every situation, will bring clarity, balance and wisdom in all things, especially those having to do with the soul and the spirit, but also our physical bodies as well. What's interesting is that the section of the chapter where we find our key verse in Hebrews 4:12 is primarily talking about the body, as it admonishes the reader not to make the mistake of ignoring the Sabbath rest to ensure the health of the body. Still, our primary goal here is to allow the Word of God to "rightly divide" the soul and the spirit so that we can have a better understanding of each. The writer of Hebrews goes on to say in the very next verse, "Nothing in all creation is hidden from God's sight. Everything is uncovered and laid bare before the eyes of him to whom we must give account." (Hebrews 4:13 NIV).

As we read the Bible, we find that in some scriptures the words *mind*, *heart*, *will*, and *thoughts* are used interchangeably, but they all are part of, or connected to, our soul. This is why the soul is the *battleground.* It's where we wrestle with following God with all of our hearts or succumbing to the temptations of the flesh. It's where we deal with lust, habits, ill intent, and pride. It's also where we are most vulnerable to fear, anxiety, stress, and worry.

This is why it's so important to be led by the Spirit, NOT by the soul. When the Spirit is in control of your soul, you experience what it means to "walk in the Spirit." When your soul is in control, it can cause you to "walk in the flesh."

The soul, as represented by the "mind" will either be "governed" and controlled by the flesh, or the Spirit. There are severe consequences in the one and tremendous blessings in the other. This is why it's so important to understand and meditate on the following scripture:

> "The mind governed by the flesh is death, but the mind governed by the Spirit is life and peace." (Romans 8:6 NIV)

So let's take a closer look at what this verse means:

> The mind (soul) governed by the flesh is *death* (stress, worry, anxiety, fear).

> The mind (soul) governed by the Spirit is *life and peace (love, peace, joy, patience . . .)*

If you are feeling overwhelmed by fear, worry, stress, and anxiety, it's likely because you are allowing your mind (soul) to be governed by and controlled by your flesh instead of the Spirit.

CHAPTER 3

THE BODY

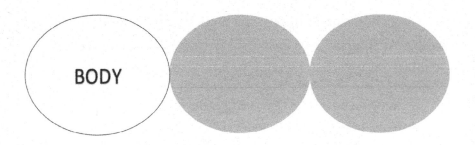

"...offer your bodies as a living sacrifice, holy
and pleasing to God—this is your true and
proper worship" (Romans 12:1b NIV)

The easiest part to identify of our tripart being is the body. Obviously, each of us has a body. This is our physical being that temporarily houses our soul and spirit. A person's physicality is the first thing we see when we meet them, and before we really get to know them.

Our bodies begin to form in the womb. After birth, they continue to grow and mature. We become larger and more developed until we reach adulthood. Barring any premature death or sickness, our physical bodies are designed to last for approximately nine decades (give or take a dozen or so years), housing our soul and spirit for our time here on earth. They then give way to physical death, releasing our spirit into the paradise that we are intended to enjoy for eternity in the presence of God. I've heard it said that our bodies are like an "earth suit," similar to a space suit. We need to wear them while we dwell on the earth; once we leave here, we can take them off because we won't need them anymore. James 2:26 tells us that "the body without the spirit is dead."

Make no mistake, our physical bodies are very important. They are the dwelling place of the Holy Spirit and the vessel God uses to establish His kingdom through us here on earth as it is in heaven.

> "Do you not know that your bodies are temples of the
> Holy Spirit, who is in you?" (1st Corinthians 6:19a).

Caring for our bodies, including physical fitness, a healthy diet, and good hygiene, is of vital importance because our bodies are the temple of the Holy Spirit. Our bodies are "fearfully and wonderfully made" (Psalm 139:14) and allow us to not only exist but also experience relationships and pleasures here on earth. The body instinctively desires and demands that its natural cravings be satisfied. Most of these cravings are inherent in our human nature as survival instincts. They include food, air, water, even reproduction, and self-protection. These God-given intrinsic tendencies are created in us to help us thrive and survive in the world. They remind us to eat, drink, automatically breathe regularly, and also to defend ourselves against internal and external threats. There is a danger however of giving in to certain cravings, habits, and inappropriate desires of the body. This is a constant battle that each person must face.

The body's natural cravings must be kept in check. Self-discipline is required to maintain moral and physical balance in our body's behaviors and tendencies. Each of us wrestles with what 1st John calls "the lusts of the flesh." These are desires to satiate cravings of the body that are excessive or inappropriate. Often, they are sexual in nature, but these lusts can also present themselves in areas such as food, intoxicants, slothfulness, hedonism, and other cravings and desires which lead to the pursuit of pleasure and sensual self-indulgence.

As important as they are, our bodies are only a small part of our person. It could be said that our body is the least important member of our trichotomy. When compared with our soul (mind and emotions), or our spirit (the spiritual part of who we are), our bodies are essentially only a superficial shell that house the rest of our being.

When getting to know someone or entering into a deep relationship with them, we will eventually find ourselves more interested in what is in their mind, heart, soul, and spirit than in their physical shell. Think about it, we only fully get to know someone by communicating with them, which usually means "talking" with them. It is quite possible to have deeper interactions with someone far away with whom we share written correspondence, electronic communication, or phone calls than it is with someone who is physically near us but with whom we have no communication. This is because we are designed to connect with others through our souls (mind/emotions) and our spirits (spiritual self). Put simply, it's not the body we form a relationship with when we truly get to know someone, but it is their soul, and ultimately their spirit.

We can only truly get to know someone's true self by looking past their physical attributes and by connecting internally to them in the soul, or even better, in the spirit. The superficial aspects of a person, while important in some respects, are not important in the deeper realms of soul and spirit. A person's height, weight, hair color, eye color, skin color, and even ethnicity are irrelevant in terms of the soul and spirit. These things are characteristics that are specific to the body. Even age, race, nationality, and gender, while they have a significant effect on a person's soul (mind/emotions/personality/influences), are still merely physical traits that belong to the body and do not clearly reflect a person's soul or spirit.

The Bible speaks very specifically about not regarding ourselves or anyone else primarily by their physical attributes (size, appearance, race, socioeconomic status, etc.). In fact, the Bible makes it very clear that God Himself looks at people differently than we see them, or even how we see ourselves or each other. We tend to regard others initially by physical appearance; God does not. He looks at the Heart.

> "Do not consider his appearance or his height, for I have rejected him. The LORD does not look at the things people look at. People look at the outward appearance, but the LORD looks at the heart." (1st Samuel 16:7 NIV)

As we study the soul and the spirit, it becomes quite clear that we are to make every effort to walk primarily in the spirit, not the soul, and certainly not the body. We will see in later chapters that satisfying the cravings of the body is called "walking in the flesh," and that our "heart" is the part of our soul (mind/emotions) that can seek God and connect to Him through our spirit by faith, which often involves denying the cravings of the body.

Walking in the Spirit requires us to *not* regard ourselves or others simply according to the body or other aspects of the physical being, but by the Spirit, which is who we are "in Christ." Read the following verse in Galatians and pay special attention to Paul's efforts to point out the various external distinctions that we are *not* to use to define ourselves or anyone else, in light of who we are in Christ Jesus. Most of these are physical or situational characteristics.

> "So in Christ Jesus, you are all children of God through faith, for all of you who were baptized into Christ have *clothed yourselves with Christ*. There is neither *Jew nor Gentile*, neither *slave nor free, nor is there male and female*, for you are all one *in Christ Jesus*." (Galatians 3:26–28 NIV)

". . . *clothed yourselves with Christ*" – no longer be identified by your outward appearance, but by Christ, whom you were baptized into.

He explains that there is neither:

- *"Jew nor Gentile" – (Ethnicity)* This does not mean that the writers of the Bible never referred to people as Jews or Gentiles; they did. It simply means that in Christ, those things do not matter. All people, regardless of religious or ethnic background, are equally given access to God through faith. Our ethnicity and race, while they still exist and may in some ways be important to our background, should not be part of our identity of who we are as new creations in Christ Jesus.

- ". . . *neither slave nor free" – (Socioeconomic)* This does not mean that everyone is the same socioeconomically. It means that we are not to value or identify anyone according to that status, only by who they are in Christ.

- "*. . . nor is there male and female*" *(Gender)* – This is *not* a statement in support of gender-neutrality. Paul is simply stating that men and women, while different physically, are the same spiritually, and equal in Christ Jesus.

When we look at each other through the "eyes of the Spirit," we see beyond physical attributes like race, ethnicity, socioeconomic status, and gender. We see people as God sees them. While we will always have physical diversity in our outward appearance, that becomes increasingly insignificant as we grow in the Spirit and become more "like Jesus." In heaven, our bodies will be different. They will be like Jesus's glorified body. The following verses tell us that we will be "like Him," and our lowly bodies will be transformed to be like His glorious body.

> "What we will be, has not yet been made known. But we know that when Christ appears, we shall be *like him*, for we shall see him as he is." (1st John 3:2b NIV).

> ". . . by the power that enables him to bring everything under his control, will transform our lowly bodies so that they will be *like his glorious body.*" (Philippians 3:21 NIV).

We don't exactly know the details of what it means to "*be like Him*," but it very possibly could mean that our bodies will be similar to the way His was after His resurrection. We will no longer be known necessarily by our particular current physical traits: height, weight, color, or appearance. We may even be like the angels in heaven, leaving our old "earth suits" far behind. Jesus explained it this way:

> "When the dead rise, they will neither marry nor
> be given in marriage; they will be like the angels in
> heaven." (Mark 12:25 NIV)

Paul writes about this incredible transformation of the body, from physical to spiritual, in his explanation of the importance of the Resurrection:

> "So will it be with the resurrection of the dead.
> The body that is sown is perishable, it is raised
> imperishable; it is sown in dishonor, it is raised in
> glory; it is sown in weakness, it is raised in power; it
> is sown a natural body, it is raised a spiritual body."
> (1st Corinthians 15:42–44 NIV)

In Revelation 7, John describes in his vision those from many diverse nations and cultures who have come out of the Great Tribulation and are now standing before the Lamb on the throne. They were *not* dressed in their own unique colors representing their different cultures. They were *not* carrying the flags of their individual nations. They were *not* speaking with many different voices in the various diverse languages that they represented. It is quite the contrary. They were all dressed identically in white robes and they all held the same thing, a palm branch. They all cried out in one voice.

> "After this, I looked, and there before me was a great
> multitude that no one could count, from every

nation, tribe, people, and language, standing before
the throne and before the Lamb. They were wearing
white robes and were holding palm branches in their
hands. And they cried out in a loud voice: 'Salvation
belongs to our God, who sits on the throne, and to
the Lamb.'" (Revelation 7:9–10 NIV)

This is a beautiful symbol of the unity that they were experiencing by coming out of the physical, and entering into the spiritual. They came from a variety of diverse cultural distinctions, and were all being welcomed into what Paul calls "one Spirit to form one body" (1st Corinthians 12:13) as they stood before the throne in the unity of the Spirit and with one voice.

Concerning ethnicity and race, sadly one of the most tragic and horrific transgressions that humankind has committed throughout history has been the mistreatment of people or other cultures primarily on the basis of their body, in other words, their outward appearance. History is full of terrible examples of mankind showing special preference toward some and hateful disdain toward others, simply by the look of their physical appearance and/or their cultural identity.

Those who walk in the Spirit have the opportunity to change this and to model to others what it looks like to do the opposite. Through the Spirit, we can be examples of people who see others as God sees them and see ourselves as God sees us. This is not to say that God is colorblind and oblivious to culture; He is not blind or oblivious to anything. He does not, however, place any emphasis or value on the color of someone's skin or their ethnicity to determine who they are in Christ and/or the condition of their soul or spirit. By looking at others from God's perspective, we can see beyond the body and all of its physical distinctives, and into the soul and the spirit, and regard people by who they truly are, not by their superficial exterior.

Several years ago, I was inspired by a comment from then presidential primary candidate Dr. Ben Carson, who echoed a similar statement that was made famous in the iconic "I have a dream" speech by Dr. Martin Luther King Jr. on the subject of race and color. When asked why he doesn't talk about race in his speeches, he responded:

> "I'm a neurosurgeon, when I take someone into the operating room, I'm actually operating on the thing that makes them who they are. The skin doesn't make them who they are." (Dr. Ben Carson)[6]

This is what it means to regard a person not simply in terms of the body, but by their soul, and also their spirit. Dr. King expressed this so powerfully with his famous words:

> "I have a dream that my four little children will one day live in a nation where they will not be judged by the color of their skin but by the content of their character." (Dr. Martin Luther King Jr.)[7]

Walking in the Spirit, and regarding people for who they are in their soul and spirit, gives us the ability to see people beyond their skin and physical features to look at the content of their character. Compared to the internal intricacies that make us who we are, the body is just a shell; the important part of a person is what's inside.

I have a friend who at a young age was in a horrific accident that left his face severely disfigured. When I first met him, it took a lot of effort for me to not think about his disfigurement as we talked, but eventually, as I got to know him, I was able to look beyond his appearance and easily engage him for who he was in his heart, soul, and personality. When I introduced him to other friends, however, I could tell that they too were initially uncomfortable, but over time were able to also look past his disfigured appearance and interact with his very extraordinary personality. I offer this example to show how easy it is to simply regard someone according to the body when God asks us to regard people according to who they are on the inside and not according to the attributes of their physical appearance.

Often our physical appearance, traits, and characteristics connect us to an identity that we are proud of. Sometimes they may even portray some ethnic distinctives that are given to us genetically and reflect our family or culture of origin. For instance, I have a distinctly Jewish nose. I never really liked it, until I began studying the Bible and realized that all of my favorite Bible heroes were also Jewish, and very likely had a similar nose (David, Solomon, Isaiah, even Jesus, and all the apostles). Now I like my nose and am proud of the Jewish heritage it links me to; however, I still must be careful not to regard myself according to my body or its particular physical features because that is *not* who I am. In Christ I cannot take pride in, or find my identity in these things; they are simply part of the shell that houses who I am in soul and spirit. I would hope that whoever desires to really get to know me would see me as God does, not the outward appearance, but the heart.

Our body *is* important however, it's the very vessel that God has given us to dwell in during our time here on earth. But to fully understand the soul and the spirit, we must look beyond the body. We must be willing to see ourselves and other people as God does, not focusing primarily on outward appearance (color, height, weight, ethnic traits, physical attributes, etc.). We need to demon-strate in our own lives, and also be examples to others of what it means to see ourselves and other people, not the way the world does with an emphasis on physical and superficial characteristics, but the way the Lord does.

> "People look at the outward appearance, but the Lord looks at the heart." (1st Samuel 16:7b NIV).

CHAPTER 4

THE SOUL

SOUL

"Bless the Lord, O my soul; and all that
is within me."(Psalm 103:1a NKJV)

The most often misunderstood part of our trichotomy is the soul.
Many people cannot clearly define what it is and what it does.
This is most likely because, from a secular perspective, it seems that
any intangible religious or even remotely spiritual subject matter is
attributed to the soul and is often called "spiritual." This is inaccurate because it is actually quite the opposite. From a purely spiritual
perspective, the soul is that part of our immaterial being that is NOT
spiritual, at least until (or unless) it is controlled by the Holy Spirit.

Even certain religious scholars hold to a dichotomous under-standing of man, conflating the soul and spirit into one. Watchman Nee addresses this as a misconception in his book *The Spiritual Man*:

> *The ordinary concept of the constitution of human beings is dualistic, soul and body. According to this concept, the soul is the invisible inner spiritual part, while the body is the visible outer corporal part. Though there is some truth to this, it is nevertheless inaccurate. Such an opinion comes from fallen man, not from God; apart from God's revelation, no concept is dependable. That the body is man's outward sheath is undoubtedly correct, but the Bible never confuses spirit and soul as though they are the same. Not only are they different in terms; their very natures differ from each other. The Word of God does not divide man into the two parts of soul and body. It treats man, rather, as tripartite; spirit, soul and body. (Watchman Nee)*[8]

The soul is simply our *mind* and *emotions*. What we think and what we *feel*. Those things can also determine our *will*, so it could be said that our soul is our mind, emotions, and in effect our will. Several studies on the soul will assert that the soul comprises three parts: mind, emotions, and will. My understanding however is that the *will* is a product of either the mind or the emotions or a com-bination of both.

Our soul is inclined to want to take control of, and attempt to govern, our entire being through the mind or emotions. Our soul is the embodiment of our thoughts and feelings. It is within the soul that we develop our intellect and learn to store and process thoughts and information. It is within our soul that we develop our psychological identity, our attractions, our tastes, our sensitivities, and our personality.

The soul is the *sole means* by which most people operate in the world. The most acclaimed scientific accomplishments or creative works throughout history were largely products of someone's soul. Your ability to be productive in your work, the basic way you interact in relationships, the most elementary way that you communicate your thoughts, and even the process by which you express your creativity in the arts are all acts of the soul. Our souls, much like our bodies, are magnificently and brilliantly created by God to give us the ability to think, feel, and live in the world. They are cerebral, emotional, visceral, and intelligent and are the basic means by which we operate in our lives and that enable us to accomplish great things, but they are *not* spiritual.

You may know some very passionate people who are deeply in touch with their feelings and emotions. They may even have the ability to express themselves so viscerally that they have a profound effect on others around them. But this is not necessarily spiritual. You may also know people who are so intellectually advanced that they can articulate the deepest concepts, even about God and scripture, and explain the complexities of things in a way that makes them appear to have superior insight into every topic and situation. But again, if this is not based on the wisdom and knowledge of God, and His presence in that person's spirit, it is not spiritual; it's only a manifestation of the soul. Until a person is made alive by the Holy Spirit, and their minds and emotions are governed by the Spirit, and *not* the flesh, they are simply operating in the soul, not the Spirit.

"These are the people who divide you, who follow
mere natural instincts and do *not have the Spirit*."
(Jude 19 NIV)

It is often within the realm of the soul that we are led into unspiritual pursuits and destructive behaviors. It is within the soul that we are vulnerable to lust and pride, and when not submitted to God's Word and directed by His Spirit, it is through the soul that we fall into sin and transgression. Only those who have the Spirit of God within them can accept and understand the things of the Spirit because they are discerned only through the Spirit.

"The person without the Spirit does not accept the
things that come from the Spirit of God but considers
them foolishness, and cannot understand them
because they are discerned only through the Spirit."
(1st Corinthians 2:14 NIV)

Why is this? Because before we believe in Jesus and are "made alive" by His Spirit, we are "dead" in the spirit.

"And you, *He made alive*, who were dead." (Ephesians 2:1a NKJV) Obviously, Paul was talking about spiritual death. The same death that we inherited due to the fall of man. Of course, our bodies weren't physically dead—they still functioned fully. Our minds and emotions were not necessarily brain-dead—we could still think and feel. But we were dead spiritually. It is not until we encounter the Holy Spirit that we experience regeneration and new life in our spirits. Once our soul is brought under the governance of the Holy Spirit, it can bless the Lord, rejoice in Him, and operate in the life and power of the Holy Spirit. This is why the Psalmist could write "Bless the Lord O my soul, and all that is within me." and Mary in her famous Magnificat could proclaim "My soul magnifies the Lord, And my spirit has rejoiced in God my Savior" (Luke 1:46–47 NKJV).

Our spiritual regeneration is the most powerful and important thing that can happen to us, and we will explore this fully when we discuss the spirit, but let's continue to focus on the soul.

As mentioned earlier, even though our souls are immaterial like our spirits, they are not any more spiritual than our bodies are. Our body and our soul are each a beautiful and necessary creation of God, but are simply mundane, meaning they serve only practical purposes, one physically and the other psychologically. So in a utilitarian sense, the body and the soul are very similar. There is, however, a very significant difference between the soul and the spirit. Even though they are both immaterial aspects of our being, they are not the same.

Understanding this important truth is the very reason I began studying the topic "soul or the spirit" years ago, and the very reason for this book. The author of Hebrews makes it clear that the Word of God is the key to being able to fully understand the difference, and rightly divide soul and the spirit.

> "For the word of God *is* living and powerful, and sharper than any two-edged sword, piercing even to the division of *soul and spirit*." (Hebrews 4:12a NKJV)

We stated earlier that the soul is simply our *mind and emotions*, what we *think* and what we *feel*. This is how we determine our *will*. Put simply, our soul is our mind, emotions, and in effect our will.

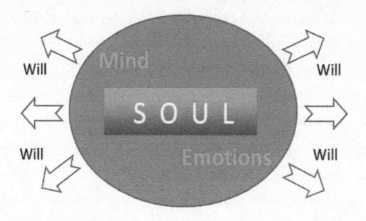

Let's take a deeper look at the mind and emotions, examining each one to see how they operate.

THE MIND

There is an ancient Hebrew saying, "The mind is the root of all conduct." It is certainly true that our minds can often drive our emotions and determine our will. A mind controlled and governed by the Spirit can accomplish great things and bring forth life and peace. A person's mind is developed even before they are born and continues to learn and grow throughout their lifetime. The brain's cerebrum, which is responsible for thinking, feeling, and memory, grows rapidly in the third trimester of pregnancy and is fully functioning by birth. At that point, the development of thoughts, feelings, voluntary actions, and reactions continues and forms the person's mental and emotional identity, also known as their personality. This is the person's soul. As it continues to grow, it will learn, it will feel, it will think, it will create, and it will even relate to other souls, but it is not spiritual. It is not operating in the realm of the spirit until that person is "made new" by the Holy Spirit.

"Be made new in the attitude of your minds."
(Ephesians 4:23 NIV)

When this happens the person becomes a new creation and the Holy Spirit is present in the thoughts, actions, and "heart" of this person. First Peter 1:9 calls this "the salvation of your souls."

"Therefore, if anyone is in Christ, he is a new creation; old things have passed away; behold, all things have become new." (2nd Corinthians 5:17 – NKJV)

Even before a person is made alive by the Holy Spirit, they can still think positive thoughts, say good things, even learn to memorize and recite spiritual content, and perhaps even recite Bible verses and prayers. But they are not operating in the Spirit; they are operating in the soul. (We will see later that the part of the soul that is acting contrary to the Spirit of God is called the "flesh.") The flesh seeks to do its own will, not God's. The flesh makes the soul vulnerable to the temptation of the enemy to act according to *his* agenda (pride and lust) and direct the will likewise.

This is why Paul tells us that it is of vital importance that the mind (soul) is controlled by the Spirit and *not* the flesh.

"The mind governed by the flesh is death, but the mind governed by the Spirit is life and peace."
(Romans 8:6 NIV)

This is very important because once our minds are governed by the Spirit, then our souls can produce spiritual fruit and are capable of being agents of the Spirit. Our minds, emotions, heart, and will all become vehicles by which the Holy Spirit works within us and operates through us.

How do we allow our minds to be governed by the Spirit?

❧ By recognizing, not ignoring, the presence of the Holy Spirit within us and choosing to allow Him to lead and guide us in His strength and power. Also by resisting the temptations and influences of the flesh.

Think of it this way: your soul is having a gubernatorial election within you. There are two candidates, "The Flesh" versus "The Spirit." One will win, and when they do, they will be the "governor" of your soul. However, there is only one voter and it's you. You have the power to choose to allow your spirit to prevail over your flesh by winning in the battleground state of the mind so that the "mind governed by the Spirit" will result in life and peace.

How do you choose who will win? These three steps from scripture will help your Spirit prevail over the flesh in the battle of the soul by having victory in the war of the mind.

1. Focus on the right things

   "Set your minds on things above, not on earthly things." (Colossians 3:2 NIV)

2. Keep your thought life under control

   ". . . take captive every thought to make it obedient to Christ." (2nd Corinthians 10:5b NIV)

3. Don't conform, be transformed

   "Do not conform to the pattern of this world, but be transformed by the renewing of your mind." (Romans 12:2a NIV)

EMOTIONS

Our emotions are given to us by God as a way to express our feelings. In fact, some may say that our emotions *are* our feelings. The most profound, visceral, and passionate thoughts within us are expressed through some type of emotion in the form of laughter, crying, shouting, groaning, sighing, and any of the various other methods that human beings emote. Some people are very emotional and expressive in the communication of their feelings; others are not as emotional but undoubtedly have the same feelings and emotions within them. Some people come from backgrounds and cultures where emotions are expressed freely and passionately. Others are raised and conditioned to express very little outward emotion of even the most deeply felt feelings. Our emotions are all built upon our inner thoughts and are a direct result of how our minds process and express data and stimuli. All of this transpires in the realm of the soul.

My family of origin is both Jewish and Italian. In some cases, there are those among my relatives who are stereotypically cerebral and headstrong and others who are extremely passionate and expressive. These attributes of the mind or emotions could in some cases be viewed as extraordinary personality traits; however, unless they are governed by the power of the Holy Spirit, they are not spiritual and are simply, as Tozer described, "soulish." Our backgrounds, ethnicities, and cultural traits can often influence the development of our souls. The way we express our emotions and articulate our thoughts are often a result of generations of ancestral tendencies that are passed down to us. These distinct characteristics are usually very beautiful and unique and often add to the mosaic that makes up the diverse array of cultures on our planet, but again, if they are merely steeped in minds and emotions, and not a direct result of

Holy Spirit–governed lives, they are simply aspects of the soul and not the spirit.

The various styles of speech, thought, and expression that we receive from our cultural backgrounds are all part of our mental and emotional DNA. Until they are controlled and governed by the Holy Spirit, they are merely soul traits of the mind and emotions, and in some cases even the flesh. That's why we mustn't confuse soulish expressions with spiritual power. Paul warns Timothy that there will be deceivers in the last days who will " *have a form of godliness but deny His power*" (2nd Timothy 3:5). Someone who speaks, sings, or simply expresses themselves passionately, or has a vast wealth of biblical knowledge and the ability to articulate it may appear to be spiritual, but may not be drawing from the Spirit of God within them, and merely operating from their soul. He wrote about himself concerning this in 1st Corinthians.

> "My message and my preaching were not with wise and persuasive words, but with a demonstration of the Spirit's power, so that your faith might not rest on human wisdom, but on God's power." (1st Corinthians 2:4-5 NIV)

Relying on wise and persuasive words instead of on the Spirit's power is something we all are tempted with. It is most apparent, however, in preachers and teachers. Many may believe that they are operating in the Spirit, but they are merely presenting the content of their soul. We've all heard speakers who were impressive and provocative in their presentation and delivery but lacked any lasting spiritual substance. Perhaps they could recite countless Bible verses and facts at will, or whip through historical data, theological concepts, or even cultural references quickly and impressively, but the sum of their presentation does not amount to any lasting spiritual impact, only many words taught by human wisdom. Paul tells us that this is not the way the Spirit speaks through us.

> "This is what we speak, not in words taught us by human wisdom but in words taught by the Spirit, explaining spiritual realities with Spirit-taught words. (1st Corinthians 2:13 NIV)

Others may operate in a manner that is very similar to persuasive politicians, salesmen, and motivational speakers, increasing and decreasing the volume, tone, and inflections of their voice to emote certain words or phrases and dramatize others in an effort to stir the senses or evoke a response in their listeners. The Bible warns us to be careful of those who manipulatively use their mental abilities or their subtle emotional tactics to make us think that we are being stirred, moved, or inspired by the Holy Spirit when we are simply reacting to a method of stimulation or provocation generated by a person's soul.

Jesus addressed this in the sermon on the mount when He told His disciples:

> "And when you pray, do not be like the hypocrites, for they love to pray standing in the synagogues and on the street corners to be seen by others. . . . do not keep on babbling like pagans, for they think they will be heard because of their many words." (Matt 6:5,7 NIV)

Jesus saw clearly that the prayers of these "hypocrites" were not a sincere pursuit of God, but merely a display of their pride. Regardless of how eloquent, and perhaps even scriptural, their words may have been, the motive was to impress and even deceive the listeners through an act of their minds and emotions, and not the Holy Spirit.

When a person is truly operating under the governance, and in the power of the Holy Spirit, instead of merely the soul, these three indicators will always be present in what they say and/or do:

1. IT WILL ALWAYS GIVE GLORY TO JESUS.

   It will not merely be a way for a person to use Jesus, or the position given to them to bring glory to themselves or direct attention elsewhere.

2. IT WILL ALWAYS BE ALIGNED WITH SCRIPTURE.

   The message will be in complete congruence with the whole message of the Word of God, not just randomly picked portions to support a particular agenda or point of view.

3. IT WILL ALWAYS BEAR FRUIT.

   Both the messenger and the message will show clear evidence of the fruit of the Spirit, and the result will be that others are brought nearer to the Lord as a result of the words or message. The response will not just be a fleeting thought or temporary emotion; it will be life-changing truth and transformative power through the Holy Spirit, not just a reaction to a display of human effort.

When a person's mind is governed by the Spirit and not just the soul, what they say and do will resonate with the Spirit of God and it will be powerful and effective because of Him. It will also carry with it the marks of the Spirit. In other words, you will always see evidence of the "the fruit of the Spirit" in the result of their ministry and also in their life as proof of the Spirit.

> "But the fruit of the Spirit is love, joy, peace, forbearance, kindness, goodness, faithfulness, gentleness and self-control." (Galatians 5:22–23 – NIV)

WALKING BY THE SOUL VS. WALKING BY THE SPIRIT

The fruit of the Spirit is not just a list of random virtues; it is the evidence of a Spirit-governed, God-centered life. Those who are not living by the Spirit of God cannot fully function in the authentic fruits of the Holy Spirit. Jesus tells us that "a bad tree cannot bear good fruit." It could be deceiving at times because sometimes things that appear to be fruits of the Spirit can seemingly be fabricated through efforts of the mind and emotions (soul), but never to the level of power and authenticity that exist when they are the genuine fruit of the Holy Spirit's presence in our lives. The first and greatest in this list of nine fruits is, of course, *love*. This is why Paul explains in 1st Corinthians 13 that someone can operate in what appears to be a highly spiritual and even sacrificial manner, but if they "do not have love," it amounts to nothing. This is likely because they are operating in the soul and not the Spirit.

> "Though I speak with the tongues of men and of angels, but have not love, I have become sounding brass or a clanging cymbal. And though I have *the gift of* prophecy, and understand all mysteries and all knowledge, and though I have all faith, so that

I could remove mountains, but have not love, I am *nothing*. And though I bestow all my goods to feed *the poor,* and though I give my body to be burned, but have not love, it profits me *nothing*." (1st Corinthians 13:1–3 NKJV)

Even those who have been made alive in the Spirit and are the *new creations* that Paul described in 2nd Corinthians 5:17, still need to be careful to not *walk according to the flesh*. We need to constantly be careful to keep our minds governed by the Spirit and not the flesh. That includes the things we think, do, and say. Otherwise, we too may find ourselves operating at times in our minds (flesh) and not the Spirit.

This is what A. W. Tozer meant when he confessed in prayer:

"It seems, Lord, that I sometimes become caught up in *soulish* expressions of worship and mistake them for spiritual worship—my spirit communing with Your Spirit."

This example is precisely what it looks like to operate in the soul, instead of the Spirit. It can happen to any of us, not just in worship, but in any of the things we think and say as well. Even as pastors and teachers, we are often tempted to rely on our own mind/intellect (soul) to bring forth a sermon or message instead of relying fully on the wisdom and power of the Holy Spirit. If we are not careful, we can easily allow ourselves to fall into a pattern of fact regurgitation from our minds, instead of speaking fresh words from the Spirit and allowing our messages to be empowered by the living, powerful Holy Spirit of God.

This could be true of all of us who teach, preach, or communicate the Word of God in any way. Whether we are a pastor, a Sunday school teacher, a worship leader, or someone who shares the gospel with friends, family, or even strangers. We must learn to *"trust in the Lord with all our heart, and lean not on our own understanding"* (Proverbs 3:5,6). I know several highly acclaimed worship leaders who have confessed that there were times when, because of circumstances or their own shortcomings, they did not operate in the power of the Spirit of God but attempted to get by with their own talent and musical skills in an effort to stimulate a spiritual response in the listeners. Sometimes it appeared to work and seemed to invoke a response in the people who received it, but it did not bear the authentic fruit and desired results that it would if they were genuinely operating and wholeheartedly living in the Holy Spirit's empowerment in both their soul *and* their spirit. Jesus taught the woman at the well that the entire pursuit of God must be *spiritual*, not merely mind and emotion.

> "God *is* Spirit, and those who worship Him must
> worship in spirit and truth." (John 4:24 NKJV)

God is not limited; however, He can use anything and anyone in any situation, regardless of their spiritual posture or state of mind. So sometimes the recipient of a ministry can still be blessed regardless of the condition of the heart of the minister. Throughout the Bible, we see how God used wicked kings, flawed messengers, and even a donkey to do His will. He is God; He can do what He wants and use whomever He wants, but the person whose mind is controlled by the flesh will always experience some sort of death in the process. Whether it is an increased insensitivity to the Spirit, a growing lack of peace, or a deeper chasm of separation with God due to the hardening of their heart. Remember, "The mind (soul) governed by the flesh is death, but the mind (soul) governed by the Spirit is life and peace."

The soul, therefore, becomes the battleground where the flesh and the spirit are in conflict with each other. We can feel the tension between the two forces competing with each other for the governance of the mind. When we allow the Spirit to govern, we have life and peace. When our mind is set on things of the flesh, we experience death and darkness.

This is also why many of us experience anxiety, worry, dissonance, and lack of peace in our lives. We often process the things we see and hear through the soul instead of through the Spirit. Many times we watch the news, read social-media posts, hear of situations, or engage in dialogues that bring us stress, worry, fear, anger, and doubt on the inside, instead of feeling God's peace and the assurance of His love. Do you ever find yourself struggling with a nagging sense of unrest, discontent, or even depression because of how the things going on in the world affect your mind and emotions? If you do, you're not alone. Many people experience these same things, especially in these times of increased information and volatile interaction. The reason you don't have peace, however, is that you are likely not walking in the Spirit; you are probably walking in the soul.

Paul has a message for you in these times:

"I say then: Walk in the Spirit, and you shall not fulfill the lust of the flesh." (Galatians 5:16 NKJV)

Walking in the Spirit is living in such a way that the Holy Spirit directs your will, actions, and even your thoughts. Walking in the flesh is simply walking in the soul because the flesh is part of the soul. It's the part that wants to please itself, instead of doing God's will. It is never satisfied however, it always craves more time, attention, and devotion to satiate its desires. It's also the part of you that is drawn to controversy, conflict, rage, and dissonance. The results of these attractions are the negative feelings that fester inside of you. Your anxiety, worry, anger, stress, dissonance, and lack of peace will never cease if you continue to walk in the soul, but these will dissipate when you walk in the Spirit. *This is why it's so important to know the difference between your Soul and your Spirit.*

The fruits of the Spirit listed in Galatians 5 (love, peace, joy, etc.) will replace those negative feelings when you walk in the Spirit. Remember what we read in Romans 8:6b: ". . . the mind governed by the Spirit is life and peace." Walking in the Spirit means having your mind governed and submitted to God's Spirit, and stayed on Him. That is what it means to trust Him. The final result is God's perfect peace in our lives. This is not just ordinary peace, it's the peace of God that passes all understanding.

> "You will keep him in *perfect peace*, Whose *mind* [soul] is stayed on You, Because he *trusts* in You." (Isaiah 26:3 NKJV)

CHAPTER 5

THE SPIRIT

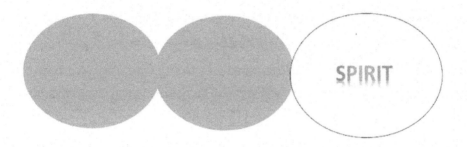

"The Spirit himself testifies with *our spirit* that we are God's children."

(Romans 8:16 NIV)

The final and most important part of our trichotomy is our spirit. It is the most important because it is the part of us where we meet God and commune with Him.

For many people, the spirit is often confused with the soul. Some people don't know that they even have a spirit or think that it and the soul are one and the same thing. This underscores the importance of the need to know how and why the Word of God "rightly divides the soul and the spirit."

> "For the word of God *is* living and powerful, and sharper than any two-edged sword, piercing even to the division of *soul and spirit*." (Hebrews 4:12a NKJV)

In every major translation of the Bible, the word "spirit" in Hebrews 4:12 is not capitalized, indicating that in this instance it is referring to the human spirit, not the Holy Spirit. In most versions, the word "Spirit" is capitalized throughout the New Testament when it is specifically referring to the Holy Spirit.

In John 4, when Jesus was speaking to the Samaritan woman at the well, He explained to her that God is *Spirit*. He also said that *we* must worship Him in *spirit* and in truth.

> "God *is* Spirit, and those who worship Him must worship in spirit and truth." (John 4:24 NKJV)

Notice the careful capitalization of "Spirit" when referring to God versus the "spirit" with which man must worship Him. Most versions of the Bible are careful to make this distinction in verses referring to the Holy Spirit as being different than the human spirit. Much has been written and studied regarding the Holy Spirit, but interestingly there is not much written on the subject of the human spirit. I hope to help the reader understand the importance of the human spirit more clearly because it is the dwelling place of the Holy Spirit within us.

WHAT IS THE SPIRIT?

A simple definition of the *spirit* – The human spirit is the internal, immaterial, nonphysical, and nonpsychological part of our being, which is potentially capable of communing with God and connecting with others in a spiritual capacity. This is the part of us where we "*meet God*" and "*commune with God*".

> ". . . it is in the realm of the spirit where man *meets God*." (Chuck Smith)[9]

> "It is by means of our spirit that we may *commune with the Spirit of God*. And it is in our spirit that we recognize the witness of the Holy Spirit." (A. W. Tozer)[10]

Although the spirit is the most important part of a person, many people don't even realize that they have a spirit because, for most people, it is inactive and dormant. In fact, the Bible says that we are spiritually dead unless we are made alive by the Spirit of the Lord.

> "As for you, you were dead . . . , But because of His great love for us, God, who is rich in mercy, made us alive with Christ." (Ephesians 2:1a,4 and 5a NIV)

Charles Spurgeon proposes that unregenerated man is made up of two parts prior to salvation: body and soul. Once he is regenerated, the "fire of God's life and love falls into his heart," and he then consists of three parts, body soul, and spirit.

> "Man in his fallen nature consists only of a body and soul, and that when he is regenerated there is created in him a new and higher nature 'the spirit' which is a spark from the everlasting fire of God's life and

love; this falls into the heart, and abides there, and makes its receiver 'a partaker of the divine nature.' Thenceforward, the man consists of three parts, body, soul, and spirit, and the spirit is the power of the three." (C. H. Spurgeon)[11]

You're probably asking, "Why would God create us with dead spirits? Aren't we created in His image? His Spirit is not dead, so why is ours?" The answer to this question is that mankind's spirits were not always dead. Spiritual death occurred during the fall of man in the Garden of Eden and has been passed on to generations ever since. The Lord gave Adam the one command to "not eat of the tree of the knowledge of good and evil." The consequence of eating from that tree was *death*.

> "And the Lord God commanded the man, saying, 'Of every tree of the garden you may freely eat; but of the tree of the knowledge of good and evil you shall not eat, for in the day that you eat of it you shall surely *die*.'" (Genesis 2:16–17 NKJV)

The death they experienced was the death of their spirits. They now were bound to living in only the realm of the soul and the body, both of which would also be subject to death after the curse. The curse of spiritual death was passed down to their descendants. Every person ever born bore the curse of spiritual death, except one, the one whose father was not human; in fact, His father was the Holy Spirit. That is the reason Jesus is the only one who can make those who are dead in spirit, alive in spirit, through His Holy Spirit. He is the way, the truth, and the life, so He can give life to our spirits.

What does it look like when someone is spiritually dead? It means that their spirits have not yet been made alive through Jesus. They may be physically healthy (body), and may also be adequately stable, both mentally and emotionally (soul), but spiritually they are dead. This is why many of our own family, friends, and loved ones have no affinity or even perception of the things of God. They may not even believe in Him and therefore are unaware and unattracted to things of the Spirit.

> "But the natural man does not receive the things of the Spirit of God, for they are foolishness to him; nor can he know *them,* because they are spiritually discerned." (1 Corinthians 2:14 NJKV)

• BEING MADE ALIVE IN THE SPIRIT

When we are born into this world, it is our natural birth, meaning that both our bodies and souls begin to grow and develop outside the womb. As we develop, our physical and emotional/mental identity is established and we operate in both realms. Our spirits, however, do not develop until we are "born of the spirit." That can only be done by being "made alive" with Christ (Ephesians 2:5). Once that happens, we begin to grow, mature, and develop spiritually as the Holy Spirit breathes life into us and God sanctifies us through and through.

> "May God himself, the God of peace, sanctify you through and through. May your whole *spirit, soul* and *body* be kept blameless at the coming of our Lord Jesus Christ." (1st Thessalonians 5:23 NIV)

Unfortunately, there are many who have not allowed God to sanctify them through and through as this verse describes because they are only aware of two-thirds of their being. Until they are "made alive" by the Spirit, their spirits are dormant, atrophied, and seemingly nonexistent because they are dead.

In the famous nighttime conversation with Nicodemus in John chapter 3 (sometimes casually referred to as "*Nic at Night*"), Jesus brings up the topic of "being born of the Spirit." He tries to explain to this highly respected, scholarly Jewish leader and teacher of the Torah that it is not possible to perceive the things of the Spirit in the same way we perceive natural things.

> "Very truly I tell you, no one can see the kingdom of God unless they are born again." "How can someone be born when they are old?" Nicodemus asked. "Surely they cannot enter a second time into their mother's womb to be born!"
>
> Jesus answered, "Very truly I tell you, no one can enter the kingdom of God unless they are born of water and the Spirit. Flesh gives birth to flesh, but *the Spirit gives birth to spirit*. You should not be surprised at my saying, 'You must be born again.' The wind blows wherever it pleases. You hear its sound, but you cannot tell where it comes from or where it is going. So it is with everyone born of the Spirit." (John 3:3–8 NIV)

Nicodemus was perplexed when Jesus told him that he must be "born again." Jesus then explained to him that this meant spiritual birth. In other words, our spirit must come alive in order to perceive things in the Spirit. Notice the usage of capitals in verse 6, "*the Spirit gives birth to spirit.*" The Holy Spirit is the one who makes our spirit come alive. Until this happens, and a person becomes born again, they are spiritually dead.

I recently spoke about this topic at an outdoor event in a popular New Jersey beach town. As an object lesson, I used three beachballs. On each of the beachballs, I had written in big bold letters the name of the tripartite entity that it represented. On the first ball, I wrote the word BODY, on the second ball I wrote the word SOUL, and on the third ball I wrote (you guessed it) SPIRIT. The only difference with the SPIRIT beachball was that, unlike the others, it was completely deflated. I invited three volunteers from the audience to come up front to help me with the demonstration. Each took one of the balls and held it up for the audience to see. I asked them to hold them close together with the BODY ball on one side, the SOUL ball in the middle, and the SPIRIT ball on the other side, representing one tripart being. Obviously, all eyes were on the deflated SPIRIT ball which looked awkward and out of place compared to the other two.

This graphic represents a person who is not yet born of the Spirit (i.e., born again) and made alive in Christ. Their spirit is completely dormant. The truth is, without the Spirit of God in that part of our being, we are spiritually dead.

Unfortunately, most people spend their whole lives this way. They can only operate and perceive things in their physical and mental capacity and are oblivious to things of the Spirit.

The good news is that Jesus freely offers everyone the opportunity to be made alive in the Spirit simply by grace through faith. We read in Ephesians that He offers us this because of His great love for us:

> "But because of His great love for us, God, who is rich in mercy, *made us alive* with Christ even when *we were dead* in transgressions—it is by grace you have been saved." (Ephesians 2:4–5 NIV)

HOW DOES IT HAPPEN?

When we become born again, repenting of our sins and unbelief, opening our hearts to fully accepting Jesus as Lord, receiving His death on the cross as the sacrifice for our sins, and submitting ourselves fully to Him, something incredible happens to us. He breathes His Spirit into our spirit, and it comes to life.

> "When you believed, you were marked in him with a seal, the promised Holy Spirit." (Ephesians 1:13b NIV)

> "He anointed us, set his seal of ownership on us, and put his Spirit in our hearts. " (2nd Corinthians 1:21b-22a NKJV)

We begin to see, hear, and feel things on a spiritual level that we have never experienced before. It's as if He breathed into a dormant chamber of our being and filled it with life. The "deflated beachball" part of us gets filled up with the *Ruach HaKodesh,* which is a Hebrew phrase that means *holy wind, breath, or Spirit of God.* It is what we call the Holy Spirit.

When this happens, our perception of the world begins to change. We no longer operate "solely in the soul" but can now perceive things through the Spirit. Our outlook on life, priorities, relationships, issues of the world, and most importantly God and His word are completely transformed. We can face tremendous hardships without anguish. We can suffer loss and disappointment without despair. We can witness the terrible events and issues that take place in the world and still maintain the peace of God because His Spirit is not only within us but also in control of us. We are no longer driven by anger, fear, jealousy, selfishness, rage, and lust. His Spirit produces within us the fruit of the Spirit (love, peace, joy, patience, kindness, goodness, gentleness, faithfulness, and self-control.)

His Spirit within us also works through us in the gifts and manifestations of the Spirit (1st Corinthians 12). We will find ourselves operating in power, wisdom, and faith that is well beyond our normal capabilities. These giftings and manifestations are not just reserved for worship and church gatherings; they enable us to operate in powers and abilities that impact the world we live in with God's power. As we learn to operate on the Spirit, instead of the soul (mind/emotions), we can see things, do things, and speak into situations at a level that is much higher and much more effective than when we could before. We become the vessels of God's Spirit here on earth. He speaks and operates through us and among us as we allow His Spirit to fill our spirit and move within us.

One way to visualize this is to imagine a human spirit as a glove. It is designed to be used in a certain way and for certain purposes. It offers no use, however, until a hand is inside of it, moving and operating within it. The human spirit is much like that glove. It can only operate if God's Spirit, His hand, is inside of it. Scripture tells us that we become not only united with Him but also "one with Him in spirit."

"But whoever is united with the Lord is one with him in spirit." (1st Corinthians 6:17 NIV)

Another very important thing that takes place when our spirits are made alive and we learn to operate in God's Spirit is that we are given spiritual wisdom and discernment. We begin to see things from God's perspective, as opposed to the deceptive smokescreens that most people are blinded with on earth. Have you ever watched a news clip, read a post, or heard some information that you sensed was suspect as if it was a falsehood or a half-truth put forth as factual, yet the people around you believed it was true? Or have you ever made a decision that you knew was God's leading but went against popular consensus? You may or may not have sensed it in your thoughts or feelings, but something deep inside you that is aligned with the Holy Spirit and the Word of God was discerning the situation on a level that other people's minds and emotions were unaware of. The Holy Spirit makes us keenly aware in our spirits of what is and what is not truth.

John tells us that we who live by the Spirit are able to recognize both the Holy Spirit and the deceptive spirits of the world.

> *"This is how you can recognize the Spirit of God: Every spirit that acknowledges that Jesus Christ has come in the flesh is from God, but every spirit that does not acknowledge Jesus is not from God. This is the spirit of the antichrist, which you have heard is coming and even now is already in the world.*
>
> *You, dear children, are from God and have overcome them, because the one who is in you is greater than the one who is in the world. They are from the world and therefore speak from the viewpoint of the world, and the world listens to them. We are from God, and whoever knows God listens to us; but whoever is not from God does not listen to us. This is how we recognize the Spirit of truth and the spirit of falsehood.." (1st John 4:2–6 NIV)*

Living by the Spirit is how you can recognize the Spirit of God, and this is also how we can recognize the Spirit of truth versus the spirit of falsehood. People whose spirits are not yet made alive, or believers who choose not to walk by the Spirit, remain blinded by the deceiver and often see and react to things according to their own understanding as opposed to God's perspective. They operate and respond in the soul, not the spirit. The results are lives filled with worry, fear, anger, and darkness as opposed to the power, love, and peace of mind that we receive from God.

"For God has not given us a spirit of fear, but of power and of love and of a sound mind." (2nd Timothy 1:7 NKJV)

SPIRITUAL WARFARE

Without the ability to "commune" with the Spirit of God, most people remain ignorant of the realm of spiritual warfare and therefore are vulnerable and unprotected in it. The enemy who operates in these realms has a heyday with people who don't even believe he's real. The spiritual forces of evil can operate very effectively in destroying the lives of people who have no perception of things of the Spirit and often doubt their existence.

Spiritual warfare takes place all around us whether we believe in it or not.

"For our struggle is not against flesh and blood, but against the rulers, against the authorities, against the powers of this dark world, and against the spiritual forces of evil in the heavenly realms." (Ephesians 6:12 NIV)

These "spiritual forces" that Paul describes are exactly what are wreaking havoc on the world in all areas. They are the reason that there is so much fear, anger, rage, violence, war, depression, and godlessness in the world. The only way to be protected against these spiritual forces is through God's strength and His spiritual armor.

"Finally, be strong in the Lord and in his mighty power. Put on the full armor of God, so that you

can take your stand against the devil's schemes."
(Ephesians 6:10–11 NIV)

This is why it is so important to not only know what the Spirit is but also be made alive in the Spirit. Otherwise, we are unable to operate in His mighty power, and in the protection of His armor. We remain powerless against the devil's schemes and could find ourselves trying to fight a spiritual battle by means of the soul (mind/emotions). On that level, we are no match for spiritual forces in heavenly realms.

In the epic film series *Star Wars*, the writers created a mysterious entity known as The Force. Those who were able to "use The Force" were not limited to natural faculties in terms of knowledge and power. They were able to operate on a superior level of power, compared to those with merely conventional knowledge and power. The power of The Force was not limited to a person's size or stature and not even an army's technical or military superiority. The Force allowed those who wielded its power to operate on such an advanced level that they were undaunted by those who did not operate in its power. Normal methods of warfare or military intelligence were ineffective against those operating in the power of The Force. As much as this example is classic sci-fi, it is loosely based on the very act of spiritual warfare that we are engaged in every day. Unlike "The Force," however, the Holy Spirit is a person with a mind, a will, and even feelings.

Since this is a spiritual battle and not a battle of minds and might, we cannot engage in it through the inferior conventional weapons of the soul. If we are drawn into battle and respond simply with our minds and emotions, we are destined for defeat. It is only through our ability to recognize what is spiritual and operate in that realm that we will find victory. We must remember however that spiritual warfare takes place constantly, not just on rare occasions. We live on the battlefield, so every day that we experience deception, bitterness, fear, anxiety, and even certain types of stress and anger is a sign that we are engaged in spiritual warfare, and the weapons of our soul (mind/emotions/will) are not enough to help us. When our spirit is in control, however, and empowered by the Holy Spirit, it will ensure our victory and bring about peace.

It is so important in the times we live in to understand how the Spirit of God fills, communes with, and dwells within our spirit because as the darkness gets darker, we are more desperate for the peace, power, and perspective of the Spirit than ever before. One of my favorite examples of this in scriptures takes place in the book of 2nd Kings. The King of Aram was pursuing the armies of Israel to destroy them. His problem was that each time he planned a secret attack, Elisha, the prophet of Israel, would supernaturally discover the plan and reveal it to the King of Israel. This enraged the King of Aram and he set his sights on chasing down Elisha to capture him.

> *"Go, find out where he is," the king ordered, "so I can send men and capture him." The report came back: "He is in Dothan." Then he sent horses and chariots and a strong force there. They went by night and surrounded the city.*

> *When the servant of the man of God got up and went out early the next morning, an army with horses and chariots had surrounded the city. "Oh no, my lord! What shall we do?" the servant asked.*

"Don't be afraid," the prophet answered. "Those who are with us are more than those who are with them."

And Elisha prayed, "Open his eyes, Lord, so that he may see." Then the Lord opened the servant's eyes, and he looked and saw the hills full of horses and chariots of fire all around Elisha.

As the enemy came down toward him, Elisha prayed to the Lord, "Strike this army with blindness." So he struck them with blindness, as Elisha had asked. (2nd Kings 6:13–18 NIV)

Elisha's servant went from being completely terrified that morning at the sight of thousands of enemy chariots and armies surrounding them, to being filled with empowerment and confidence as his eyes were open to see the hills full of horses and chariots of fire of the Lord's angel armies protecting them all around. Elisha simply prayed, "Open his eyes, Lord, so that he may see," and he saw.

This is what we experience when we operate in the Spirit and not the soul. The soul, apart from the spirit, is only aware of what the mind and emotions are able to perceive. The Spirit, however, gives us the advantage of seeing things as God sees them and the ability to respond in His wisdom and His power. This is what it means to "live in the Spirit" and "walk in the Spirit."

"If we *live in the Spirit*, let us also walk in the Spirit." (Galatians 5:25 NKJV)

WALKING IN THE SPIRIT

"So I say, walk by the Spirit, and you will not gratify the desires of the flesh. For the flesh desires what is contrary to the Spirit, and the Spirit what is contrary to the flesh. They are in conflict with each other" (Galatians 5:16-17b NIV)

The truth is that when you walk in the Spirit, filled with His Spirit, guided by His wisdom, and empowered by His strength, you will have victory in the battle of the soul and will find yourself no longer bound to living just to gratify the desires of the flesh. Walking in the Spirit means seeking Him first above all things. Submitting your will to His, confessing your weakness, operating in His power, and being available to do what He directs you to do and go where He leads you to go.

If you walk in the Spirit in this way, watch what happens. You'll notice that your mind becomes governed and controlled by the Spirit, and you will not gratify the desires of the flesh.

CHAPTER 6

THE FLESH AND
THE HEART

"The mind governed by the *flesh* is hostile
to God." (Romans 8:7a NIV)

"For it is with your *heart* that you believe and
are justified." (Romans 10:10a NIV)

The *soul* has two agents working within it. One with a propensity
to pursue selfish desires and the other with the potential for
pleasing God. These two agents are known as the "Flesh" and the
"Heart." These two terms, the *flesh* (*Gr. sarkos*) and the *heart* (*Gr.
kardia*), become a bit of a misnomer in modern English because
when they are used in a different context, they are both names for
material parts of the body, yet they are also used in scripture as
names for immaterial manifestations of the soul. It can be confusing,
so we must remember the context in which both these words are
being used. The immaterial flesh and heart are both driven by the
mind and emotions and are manifest in the will.

> "For the word of God *is* living and powerful, and
> sharper than any two-edged sword, piercing even
> to the division of soul and spirit, and of joints and
> marrow, and is a discerner of the *thoughts and intents*
> of the heart." (Hebrews 4:12 NKJV)

According to scripture, the *flesh* is the part of our soul that wants to please the body and is in constant conflict with our spirit. It pulls away from the things of God and is only concerned with satiating and satisfying the cravings of the body, physically, mentally, and even emotionally.

> "For the flesh desires what is contrary to the Spirit,
> and the Spirit what is contrary to the flesh. They are
> in conflict with each other, so that you are not to do
> whatever you want." (Galatians 5:17 NIV)

The *heart* is the part of our soul that wants to please and commune with God through the spirit. It is with the heart that we exercise faith, by believing in God in our hearts.

> "If you confess with your mouth the Lord Jesus and
> *believe in your heart* that God has raised Him from
> the dead, you will be saved." (Romans 10:9 NKJV)

Since the flesh and heart both reside within the realm of the soul, their intentions are driven by our mind and emotions and manifest in our will. They are in constant struggle with each other, however, over our will. The flesh is intent on satiating the cravings and desires of the body, while the heart has the capacity to believe unto righteousness, thus opening the doorway to the spirit and creating a faith connection by which the spirit comes alive and takes control.

The flesh represents the propensity toward selfishness, while the heart represents the potential for love. Selfishness is in essence the desire to please oneself rather than care for or have concern for the welfare of others. Love is very different because it desires what's best for the other, regardless of the benefit or consequences to itself. *Love is the opposite of selfishness*; therefore the *flesh* is the opposite of the *heart*.

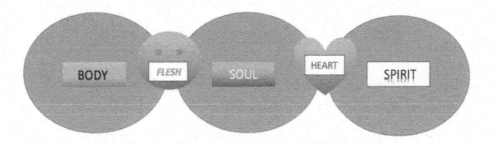

Have you ever witnessed or been involved in a game of tug-of-war? This is an internationally popular sport that pits two opposing teams against each other in a contest of strength. Each team holds on tightly to a thick rope and competes by pulling firmly on the rope. The teams strain against each other with tremendous tension on the rope until one team prevails by pulling the rope, and the other team a certain distance toward them, therefore gaining dominance and victory.

The dynamic within the soul is very much like that. The adversarial forces are the flesh, represented by the sinful nature, and the Spirit, represented by the heart. The flesh is primarily concerned with pleasing and gratifying the body and the sinful mind. The heart has the ability to believe and connect to the Spirit through faith and therefore pulls the entire soul in the direction of the Spirit. The soul bears the strain of the tension between the two forces just as the rope does in the game of tug-of-war. The flesh pulls one way toward the cravings and lusts of the body, and the heart pulls the other way, believing in and submitting to the Spirit. The result is exactly what Paul was referring to when he wrote, "For the flesh desires what is contrary to the Spirit, and the Spirit what is contrary to the flesh. They are in conflict with each other."

He explained the struggle of the mind in more detail in the book of Romans:

> "Those who live according to the flesh have their
> minds set on what the flesh desires, but those who
> live in accordance with the Spirit have their minds
> set on what the Spirit desires." (Romans 8:5 NIV)

The struggle is real. There are spiritual forces at play to try to keep our mind set on the flesh. This is why the defense must also be spiritual and not just mental and emotional. We are in a spiritual battle where the enemy tries to tempt us and deceive us according to our weaknesses. On the night of the last supper, Jesus warned the apostles, "Satan has asked to sift each of you like wheat." Temptation was near; they needed to remain vigilant in the spirit, and not weak in the flesh. This is why Jesus warned them later that evening:

> "Watch and pray so that you will not fall into
> temptation. The spirit is willing, but the flesh is
> weak." (Matthew 26:41 NIV).

Paul described the struggle as a "war within" in Romans. He uses the term "inner being" to describe his Spirit, and the phrase "law of sin" to describe the flesh. He also uses the phrase "law of my mind" to describe his soul.

> "So I find this law at work: Although I want to do good, evil is right there with me. For in my inner being I delight in God's law; but I see another law at work in me, waging war against the law of my mind and making me a prisoner of the law of sin at work within me. What a wretched man I am! Who will rescue me from this body that is subject to death?" (Romans 7:21–24 NIV)

Much like in the laws of physics, there is always tension. The law of gravity dictates that everything must be pulled down to earth; however, Newton's laws of motion show us that velocity, acceleration, and inertia can cause an object to fly. It doesn't defy the law of gravity; it operates in tension with it. This is very similar to the tension that exists between the flesh and the heart in the battle of soul and spirit. Every one of us experiences the constant struggle with sin that Paul describes in his own personal confession in Romans 7.

Make no mistake, however, it is not just an internal struggle of the mind that can be overcome by "mind over matter" or "self-will." It is a spiritual battle that is waged in the battle zone of the mind. The soul is the territory being fought over. The adversaries at war are the flesh and the heart. The objectives of the flesh are to fulfill the desires that are contrary to those of the Spirit. The heart, when connected to the Spirit by faith, is determined to fulfill God's desires and to bring the whole body, soul, and spirit into the sanctification of the God of peace.

> "Now may the God of peace Himself sanctify you completely; and may your whole spirit, soul, and body be preserved blameless at the coming of our Lord Jesus Christ." (1st Thessalonians 5:23 NKJV)

Secular psychoanalysts have studied the mind for years to try to determine what drives people to good, bad, and other behaviors. Sigmund Freud, who is considered the father of psychoanalysis, theorized that much like the soul, the human mind comprises three main parts: Id, Superego, and Ego. According to his psychoanalytic theory, as described in his famous book *The Ego and the Id,* on one side of the mind, the id is the instinctual part of the mind and the source of sexual and aggressive drives. The superego on the other side is the moral conscience that maintains the ethics and social standards of its environment. The ego is in the middle, basically acting as the mediator between the two. Sort of like a common scenario we see in old cartoons: a character has a devil on one shoulder and an angel on the other, each trying to tempt or influence the character's decision.

Freud's theory is widely accepted in secular psychology; however, the cartoon scenario is probably more consistent with the Word of God because the struggle is not simply isolated within the human mind. There are spiritual forces whose schemes and machinations are working hard to tempt and influence us every day. There are also worldly forces that are controlled by those spiritual forces that try to influence us every day. The battle is not won simply by allowing our ego to choose our superego over our id, or by simply exercising control over the impulses of our minds. The battle is won by having our minds governed by the Spirit and set on what the Spirit desires.

> "Those who live in accordance with the Spirit have their minds set on what the Spirit desires. The mind governed by the flesh is death, but the mind governed by the Spirit is life and peace." (Romans 8:5b–6 NIV)

THE FLESH

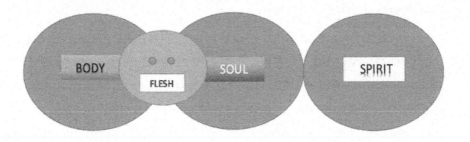

"For I know that in me (that is, in my flesh) nothing good dwells." (Romans 7:18a NKJV)

The flesh is in essence our *sinful nature*. This is the part of us with a proclivity and desire to not only disobey God but also live contrary to the Spirit.

It can be confusing because in some verses in the Bible, the word *flesh* refers to the physical human body or the actual skin or meat of a person or an animal. In the verses above and others within the same context, the flesh is the name given to the part of the soul that is specifically intent on gratifying the cravings of the body and the sinful mind. These cravings can be anything, from natural survival instincts like eating, mating, and protecting, to what is described in 1st John as "the lust of the eyes, the lust of the flesh and the pride of life."

Each of us struggles with our fallen nature to some extent. Our body's cravings need to be kept in control and the thoughts in our minds need to be taken captive. This is the conflict between the flesh and the Spirit that Paul describes in Galatians 5:17. He finishes that verse with the words "The Spirit [desires] what is contrary to the flesh. They are in conflict with each other, so that you are not to do whatever you want." While the body may have many cravings and behavioral tendencies, the flesh (sinful nature) that governs those tendencies resides in the soul.

Genesis tells us that God created man in His own image and saw that it was very good. Even our souls are created in His image. Our ability to think, feel emotion, and be creative are all marks of our maker. Our flesh, however, is vulnerable to the temptation to crave *more than* or *other than* what God has for us. Adam and Eve were perfectly provided for in the Garden of Eden. They had all that they needed and everything they desired. The serpent, however, tempted them to desire *more than* and *other than* what God had provided. Their desire to eat from the tree of the knowledge of good and evil and the disobedience that followed was an act of the *flesh*, not just the body.

Our bodies are created with many tendencies and cravings, along with the ability to exercise self-control. Eating is not a sin, but overeating can be. Beverages and medicine are not sinful, but overindulgence in certain beverages and harmful drugs can lead to death. The body has its desires and cravings (air, food, water, etc.), but the flesh causes the body to crave and indulge in the objects of its desires in an unacceptable or inappropriate manner. This includes every area where the flesh is manifest: sexuality, pride, envy, self-image, language, truthfulness, thoughts, communication, food, intoxicants, etc. The flesh is entirely self-seeking and not God-pleasing. This is why Paul tells us in Romans 8:

> "The mind governed by the flesh is death, but the mind governed by the Spirit is life and peace. The mind governed by the flesh is hostile to God; it does not submit to God's law, nor can it do so. Those who

are in the realm of the flesh cannot please God."
(Romans 8:6–8 NIV)

In this important verse in our study, Paul points out the dangers of having our mind (soul) governed or controlled by the flesh (our sinful nature). Hostility toward God and rejection of Him and His word are rooted in a soul that is governed by the flesh. Those who operate in this way cannot please God. This means that insomuch as we are being directed, influenced, and motivated by things other than God, we cannot please God. In fact, the only way we can truly please God is by faith. The only way to exercise faith is by believing, and that is done not through *flesh*, but with the *heart*.

> "Without faith, it is impossible to please God because anyone who comes to him must believe." (Hebrews 11:6a NIV)

THE HEART

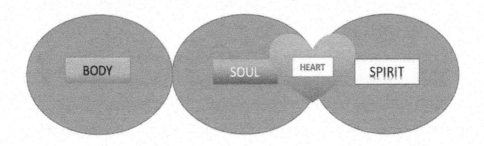

> "For with the heart one believes unto righteousness." (Romans 10:10a NKJV)

The *heart* is another often misunderstood part of our being. First, we must clarify that we are obviously not talking about the internal muscular organ in our chest that pumps blood through our circulatory system. The Bible mentions the word *heart* nearly one thousand times. Most, but not all, are referring to our deepest emotions that direct our thoughts and actions toward someone or something else. It's the vehicle by which we exercise faith, trust, and love. It's important to note, however, that our hearts can also be directed toward evil. Jesus Himself observed that the heart of man is inclined toward evil and said, "From within, out of the heart of man, come evil thoughts." In fact, in one of the saddest moments in the entire Bible, God saw that man's heart had become so evil that He decided to destroy the earth by flood.

> "The Lord saw how great the wickedness of the human race had become on the earth, and that every inclination of the thoughts of the human heart was only evil all the time." (Genesis 6:5 NIV)

The heart is very important in this context because it is the part of our soul that gives us the ability to *believe* or exercise faith which connects our soul to our spirit. By "believing in our heart" our spirit is "made alive" by God's Spirit.

This process is sometimes called "regeneration." It is basically the process of being born again. It's one of many terms and phrases used to describe a person who has come to believe in Jesus as Lord and become saved by grace through faith in Jesus's death and resurrection for the forgiveness of sins..

The Bible gives us clear instructions on how to be saved, but it is predicated not just on what we say but also on our willingness to believe *with our hearts.*

"If you confess with your mouth the Lord Jesus and believe in your heart that God has raised Him from the dead, you will be saved. For with the heart one believes unto righteousness." (Romans 10:9–10a NKJV)

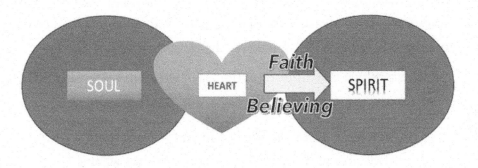

The beautiful thing that takes place when we believe with our hearts is that our spirits become alive because of the presence of His Spirit within us, as we welcome Him into our hearts. That same Spirit affirms this experience by exclaiming the words, "Abba Father."

"God sent the Spirit of his Son into our hearts, the Spirit who calls out, 'Abba, Father.'" (Galatians 4:6b NIV)

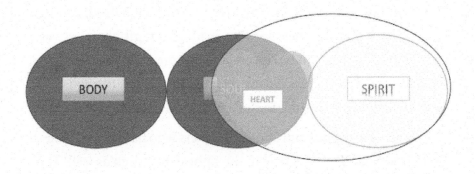

Unfortunately, many people have not had this experience, and are not yet born again. They have not been regenerated and have yet to experience salvation by believing in their hearts, so they, therefore, have not had their spirits "made alive." They spend their whole lives "walking in the flesh," and *not* the Spirit. The results are what we see permeating the world around us, including sexual immorality, impurity, lustful pleasures, idolatry, hostility, quarreling, jealousy, outbursts of anger, selfish ambition, dissensions, division, and envy.

This is why it is so important that each one of us believes *in our hearts* so that we *can* walk in the Spirit and not the flesh.

> "So I say, *walk by the Spirit*, and you will not gratify the desires of the flesh. For the flesh desires what is contrary to the Spirit, and the Spirit what is contrary to the flesh. They are in conflict with each other, so that you are not to do whatever you want. But if you are led by the Spirit, you are not under the law. The acts of the flesh are obvious: sexual immorality, impurity, and debauchery; idolatry and witchcraft; hatred, discord, jealousy, fits of rage, selfish ambition, dissensions, factions." (Galatians 5:16–20 NIV)

This ominous list of words in Galatians 5:19-20 describes most people in the world. This is why there is so much hatred, conflict, pride, greed, and darkness in the world. Every problem between people in the world can be traced back to some sin, or an instance where someone who, like Adam, decided to exercise the will of the flesh instead of submitting to the will of God's Spirit.

We all have friends and family members who have yet to "believe in their hearts." This was true in the Ephesian church as well. They were spiritually dead until they were made alive by believing in their hearts.

> *And you He made alive, who were dead in trespasses and sins, in which you once walked according to the course of this world, according to the prince of the power of the air, the spirit who now works in the sons of disobedience, among whom also we all once conducted ourselves in the lusts of our flesh, fulfilling the desires of the flesh and of the mind, and were by nature children of wrath, just as the others. But God, who is rich in mercy, because of His great love with which He loved us, even when we were dead in trespasses, made us alive together with Christ. (Ephesians 2:1–5a NKJV)*

Without "believing in their hearts" and having their spirits *made alive* through the Holy Spirit dwelling within them, a person cannot walk by the Spirit. Most people are doomed to a life of walking only in the flesh. That's why we see Romans 8:6 play out in real life over and over again: "The mind governed by the flesh is death, but the mind governed by the Spirit is life and peace."

It's important to know that the heart is not just the means by which we welcome the Spirit into our lives when we first believe; it's the *ongoing channel by which we continue to live by the Spirit* as opposed to living a life controlled by the flesh. The writer of Hebrews reminds us of the warning found in Psalm 95,

> "Today, if you hear his voice, do not harden your hearts." (Hebrews 4:7b NIV)

We are faced daily with the choice of trusting the Lord with our hearts (Spirit) or simply trusting our own understanding (soul).

Solomon offers some very wise advice, encouraging us to "trust" (*have faith in*) the Lord with all of our hearts, and not just rely on our limited cognitive understanding.

> "Trust in the Lord with all your <u>heart</u>, and lean not
> on your own understanding." (Proverbs 3:5 NIV)

He uses the phrase "all of your *heart*" as an exhortation for us to trust in the Lord with every part of our being. The heart can direct both our mind *and* emotions toward the Lord. There is a danger in pursuing God "half-heartedly," which means trusting Him only with the things we understand but not trusting him with the things we don't. Trust and faith are the exact same word in the New Testament. They are both translated from the Greek word *pistis*. In fact, the word *faith* can be replaced by the word *trust* in just about every verse in the New Testament and the meaning of the verse would not be altered in any way. *Faith* sounds a bit more religious and *trust* sounds a bit more relational, but the meaning stays the same. By trusting the Lord with all of our hearts, we are putting our faith fully in Him. Remember Hebrews 11:6: ". . . without faith it is impossible to please God."

THE GREATEST COMMANDMENT

When Jesus was asked what the "Greatest Commandment" was, He responded that we are to love God with everything we've got, and to do it "heart first," meaning with our deepest desires and trust.

> "One of the teachers of the law came and heard them
> debating. Noticing that Jesus had given them a good
> answer, he asked him, "Of all the commandments,
> which is the most important?" "The most important

one," answered Jesus, "is this: 'Hear, O Israel: The Lord our God, the Lord is one. Love the Lord your God with all your *heart* and with all your *soul* and with all your *mind* and with all your *strength*." (Mark 12:28–30 NIV)

He was literally quoting from the book of Deuteronomy in the Torah, which includes two very common Jewish prayers that are still recited in synagogues every Shabbat. The first is the Shema, which says, "Shema Yisrael Adonai Elohenu, Adonai Echad," and then continues with another prayer known as the V'ahavta, which includes the words "V'ahavta et Adonai Elohecha B'chol l'vavcha, uv'chol nafshecha uv'chol me'odecha" (transliterated Hebrew).

All of this is a direct quote from Deuteronomy 6, which says:

> "Hear, O Israel: The Lord our God, the Lord *is* one! You shall love the Lord your God with all your *heart*, with all your *soul*, and with all your *strength*." (Deuteronomy 6:4–5 NIV)

Luke's and Mark's accounts of the Greatest Commandment include the word *strength*. All of them, however, start with the phrase "you shall love the Lord your God with all your *heart*."

Heart – Deepest desires, and the ability to believe.

Soul – Mind and emotions that can determine our will.

Mind – Thoughts, intellect, and ability to reason.

Strength – Physical abilities, might, and energy.

Jesus said that we need to love God with every part of our soul and our physical strength as well. When we do that, something supernatural happens. The "eyes of our heart" are opened and we believe. When this occurs, the Holy Spirit is welcomed to come in and fill our human spirits and His Spirit and the eyes of our hearts are enlightened.

EYES OF YOUR HEART

"I pray that the *eyes of your heart* may be enlightened in order that you may know the hope to which he has called you, the riches of his glorious inheritance in his holy people." (Ephesians 1:18 NIV)

Paul prays this beautiful prayer at the beginning of his letter to the Ephesian church after an extensive run-on sentence, where he prays for this young church plant to experience every blessing and promise that God has for them. He knows that in the natural (that is, in the physical and soulish realm), they would not be able to see the glorious riches to which they have been called. In fact, the hope and promises that God intended for them would be obscured by the physical and temporal distractions and circumstances that they were entrenched in.

This is exactly how it is with us. Without the eyes of our "heart" enlightened, we only see darkness. Our heart is the part of our soul that has the unique ability to have faith and trust in God even when we mentally or emotionally cannot. Our heart is not just the bridge between our soul and our spirit, it's the *conduit* that joins these two parts of our tripart being, allowing the Spirit to permeate, move through, and *take control of our souls*. Paul continues his prayer in chapter 3, praying that Christ may dwell in our hearts through faith."

"I pray that out of his glorious riches He may strengthen you with power through his Spirit in your inner being, so that Christ may dwell *in your hearts through faith.*" (Eph 3:16–17a NIV)

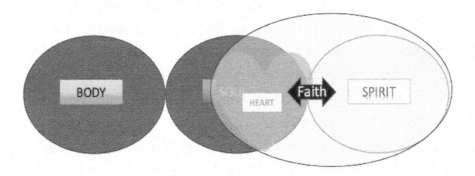

When we understand the importance of the heart and allow the *eyes of our hearts* to be enlightened by the Holy Spirit within us, we will begin to see things through the Spirit, NOT just what is presented to us in the natural.

We will have supernatural wisdom to recognize truth and sense deception, whether it be on the news, through social media, or through other information presented to us daily.

We will have God's perspective on politics, world issues, justice, economics, health, relationships, sexuality, finances, etc.

We will have peace, joy, patience, and self-control within us, even in the face of severe tension and conflict all around us.

Why aren't more people experiencing this now? It is because in our human nature we have the tendency to only "see through the eyes of the soul" and not through the "eyes of the heart" (Spirit). There is a huge difference.

This is why it is so important to know the difference between the soul and the spirit, and also to be able to distinguish clearly the difference between the *Flesh* and the *Heart*.

If you feel consumed with worry, stress, anger, anxiety, or fear from the things you see and hear all around you, it doesn't mean you are not a believer; it just means that you may need help in areas of your unbelief. Jesus encountered a desperate father of a boy who was under regular attack by an evil spirit. This evil spirit would manifest itself with symptoms similar to epilepsy and had also robbed the boy of his speech. The father was a believer in Jesus, yet he struggled with unbelief. The condition of his son, and perhaps some other struggles in his life, had led to a deficiency in his faith. Jesus spoke to him about believing, and his response was so humble and genuine that it moved the Lord to immediately take action on his behalf. The father's words were:

> "I do believe; help me overcome my unbelief." (Mark 9:24b NIV).

Sometimes *we* need to pray this prayer as well. When we see the world crumbling all around us, and people we love suffering, our faith can be shaken. We need God's help to overcome our unbelief and to see things from His perspective, not our own. If we feel this way, we can ask God to "open the eyes of our heart," or, as Paul prayed, "that the *eyes of your heart may be enlightened.*"

He can give us the spiritual vision that comes when *our spirit* is indwelled with the *Holy Spirit.* He can give us wisdom, knowledge, power, and understanding of God, instead of whatever limited knowledge and perception we have on our own. We begin to see things from *His perspective*, not the world's. As a result, we can have confidence, peace, joy, and comfort that we cannot attain any other way.

If we want the Spirit to open the eyes of our hearts, we must *believe in Him, trust in His Word,* and *pray.*

- Believe in His power and authority over any power or authority on Earth.

- Trust His Word above anything you read or hear.

- Pray that He will enlighten your vision and understanding so that you will know what is real and what is true according to His Spirit, and also what is not.

CHAPTER 7

LIVING IN THE SPIRIT

"If we *live in the Spirit*, let us also walk in
the Spirit." (Galatians 5:25 NKJV)

"Living in the Spirit," which is also called "walking in the Spirit," simply means being controlled, governed, directed, and motivated by the Spirit of God above all things. That means directing our will to choose the Spirit above the soul and its thoughts and feelings, and certainly above the body with its cravings and desires. Theoretically, it means that the Spirit is the head of our being and the other two parts basically support the head. Up until now, for the purpose of our tripartite explanation, we have used a lateral illustration of body–soul–spirit, similar to an ant with a head, thorax, and an abdomen.

For most of our illustrations going forward, we will present this diagram vertically like a snowman instead of laterally like an ant. The Spirit will be on top, with the soul and body supporting it from beneath. This demonstrates the importance of the Spirit as the "head" of our being and the other parts underneath it in support of it, and under its governance.

This vertical diagram represents a person who is living by the Spirit. They are in effect governed by the Spirit instead of being led by the body or soul. It's vitally important that we learn to operate under this structure of living by the Spirit, and NOT according to the flesh (soul/body). Having our whole being governed by the Spirit is the only way for us to fully experience God's will in our lives, which brings true life and real peace.

> "Those who live according to the flesh have their minds set on what the flesh desires, but those who live in accordance with the Spirit have their minds set on what the Spirit desires. The mind governed by

the flesh is death, but the mind governed by the Spirit
is life and peace." (Romans 8:5–6 NIV)

Sometimes we start out walking in the Spirit, trusting in God's power and wisdom, but then find ourselves tempted to revert to a habit of relying on our own resources and self-sufficiency, operating in the flesh instead of the Spirit. This is an example of "walking in the soul," instead of "walking in the Spirit." If we're not careful we become like the "foolish Galatians" who started out being led by the Spirit but tried to continue and finish by means of the flesh, in other words, the soul.

> "Are you so foolish? After beginning by means of the
> Spirit, are you now trying to finish by means of the
> flesh?" (Galatians 3:3 NIV)

GOD IS SPIRIT

But there's more to it. Paul goes on to say that unless we have the Spirit of Christ, we do not belong to Him. That's right, having the Spirit, being led by the Spirit, and living by the Spirit is not just an optional preference for Christians who like to refer to themselves as "Spirit-filled." It's for all who consider themselves children of God. It's only through the Spirit that we receive the adoption that makes us sons and daughters of God.

> *You, however, are not in the realm of the flesh but are*
> *in the realm of the Spirit, if indeed the Spirit of God*
> *lives in you. And if anyone does not have the Spirit of*
> *Christ, they do not belong to Christ . . .*

For those who are led by the Spirit of God are the children of God. The Spirit you received does not make you slaves, so that you live in fear again; rather, the Spirit you received brought about your adoption to sonship. And by Him we cry, "Abba, Father." The Spirit himself testifies with our spirit that we are God's children. (Romans 8:9,14–16 NIV)

Being children of God is a spiritual experience. It is not simply a religion, philosophy, persuasion, or even a lifestyle. It's a relationship, but it is not a mental, an intellectual, or even an emotional relationship. God is Spirit; there is no other way to fully experience Him than through the Spirit.

Jesus met a woman in Samaria who was culturally different from Him. Not only was she not a Jew but she was also a woman. She was a Samaritan, which meant she did not believe in anything beyond the writings of Moses. None of the writings of the prophets or even the kings and psalmists meant anything to her. She had been through multiple marriages and relationships and was seemingly ostracized by her community. She was alone at the well looking for the most natural thing in the world, water. Jesus offered her the most *supernatural* thing in the world, the Holy Spirit. Listen to what He says to her about God and those who seek Him:

> "But the hour is coming, and now is, when the true worshipers will worship the Father in spirit and truth; for the Father is seeking such to worship Him. *God is Spirit,* and those who worship Him must worship in *spirit* and truth." (John 4:23–24 NKJV)

God is Spirit, and true worshippers must worship in spirit (and in truth). We don't have a choice. If we want to worship God, or even seek, follow, serve, or believe in God, we must do it through the spirit, because He is Spirit. The Bible also tells us that God is light, and the only way to have fellowship with Him is by walking in His light. This can only be done through our regenerated spirit. it is not accomplished merely through the body or the soul.

> "God is light; in Him there is no darkness at all. If we claim to have fellowship with him and yet walk in the darkness, we lie and do not live out the truth. But if we walk in the light, as he is in the light, we have fellowship with one another, and the blood of Jesus, his Son, purifies us from all sin." (1st John 1:5b–7 NIV)

POWER IN THE SPIRIT

One very important aspect of life in the Spirit is power. Jesus chose His last and final words to His apostles very carefully. He could have said anything to them just before He was taken up in the ascension. He had traveled with them for three and a half years, teaching them, revealing things to them, telling parables, interpreting the Hebrew scriptures for them, and even explaining to them things about the kingdom that they didn't fully understand. But now He was about to vanish from their sight and they would have to live out the rest of their lives with His final words ringing in their ears. What were those words? They were words about a promise of something new that was about to begin.

Jesus's final words before the ascension were:

> "But you will *receive power* when the *Holy Spirit*
> comes on you; and you will *be my witnesses* in
> Jerusalem, and in all Judea and Samaria, and to the
> ends of the earth." (Acts 1:8 NIV)

We should never underestimate the importance of these words. The power of the Holy Spirit changed everything. No longer were the apostles watching Jesus operate in the power of the Holy Spirit, while they stood by as spectators. They would receive it too. This would give them the power to operate way beyond the abilities of their souls—this was the power of His Spirit within them. This took place in Acts 2 when they were filled with the Holy Spirit on Pentecost.

Without that power, they would not have the wisdom, boldness, and supernatural abilities to bring the gospel to thousands of people in their generation, which has extended to billions of people throughout history. They would not have been able to perform the miracles they did and wouldn't have had the supernatural wisdom and knowledge to write the entirety of the New Testament through the divine inspiration of the Holy Spirit. They would have been limited to their bodies and souls, which would merely have been their own human abilities, resources, faculties, and whatever they could conjure up in their minds and retain in their memories.

This is true of all of us. We may have talents, abilities, educated minds, and perhaps even exceptional giftedness. But without the power of the Holy Spirit working through us, we are severely limited in the impact and effectiveness that we have in the ministry God has for us. We are also powerless to face the challenges and opposition that come against us every day of our lives.

We need the power of the Holy Spirit to "be His witnesses," but also to be able to navigate through the treacherous roads of life that we all are journeying on.

For one of my visits to Nashville, I made arrangements to pick up a rental car from the airport. I had reserved the cheapest car I could find that would fit my family of four, but when I arrived at the desk, the agent told me that there were no more economy cars available but was willing to upgrade me at no extra charge. He offered me a brand-new Jeep Cherokee Trail Hawk. I'm not a *Jeeper*, but it sounded like a good deal so I took it. It seemed like it would be a lot more fun than the small economy car we usually rented. When I got into the driver's seat, I saw what makes Jeeps so special. They have POWER that regular cars don't have. In fact, there is a whole section of the dashboard called "Power." This panel consisted of buttons and controls for settings I had never seen in a regular car that allowed the driver to engage the four-wheel-drive system in a variety of modes. There were options for snow, sand, mud, and rock. There was even a button called "water-fording," which apparently enabled it to drive through rivers, I suppose.

I wish I could say that I drove the Jeep through mountainous terrains, deep valleys, mud, and rivers during our trip to Tennessee, but I didn't. We basically stayed on the roads and in parking lots. The point is, I could have traveled through some of the difficult terrain described by the dashboard buttons had I needed to, because the jeep was equipped with extraordinary "POWER."

This is what it's like to operate in the Spirit, as opposed to the soul. It's not just a spiritual display, it's real power to get us through the tough moments in life that we all face. It's wisdom in a storm of confusion. It's perseverance when everything within us wants to give up. It's joy when we have no circumstantial reason to be happy, or to even be content. And it's the power of the Holy Spirit speaking, working, and operating through us in ways that we could never do on our own.

Ultimately, the power of the Holy Spirit is meant to help us preach the gospel and be His witnesses to the world, but it is also intended to give us power to get us through the struggles of *everyday life*.

Just living in this world can deplete and discourage us *Physically*, *Mentally*, *Emotionally*, and even *Spiritually*. We need the Holy Spirit's power in all four areas.

1. <u>Physically</u>: So many people I know are worn out. We keep schedules that pack more into a twenty-four-hour period than the human body was ever created for. We may not "labor in the fields" as much as generations before us who worked hard every day from sunup to sundown, but we fill our time with nonstop activities that drain us physically and wear us out more than we were ever meant to be. The results are often stress, sickness, and sometimes chemical dependence just for relief. The Holy Spirit's power extends even to our mortal bodies, giving us life and rejuvenation.

   "But if the Spirit of Him who raised Jesus from the dead dwells in you, He who raised Christ from the dead will also give life to your mortal bodies through His Spirit who dwells in you." (Romans 8:11 NKJV)

2. Mentally: The Information Age has created an unsustainable demand for the attention of our minds. We are constantly bombarded and inundated with not just information but also interaction. As a result, our minds are usually completely exhausted because they get no rest. The access to nonstop interactive information through our phones and other devices keeps us constantly "on," and we are continually being drained of power. We become mentally depleted that we don't even have the strength to pray. The Holy Spirit within us prays for us and through us with words that our minds don't even have to think about.

"In the same way, the Spirit helps us in our weakness. We do not know what we ought to pray for, but the Spirit himself intercedes for us through wordless groans." (Romans 8:26 NIV)

3. Emotionally: Constant access to an enormous amount of electronic information keeps us continually engaged in emotionally draining situations. News of tragedies, deaths, illnesses, injustice, etc., flood our emotions daily and keep us sad, angry, frustrated, or disappointed. The Holy Spirit within us replaces those negative emotions with His responses in what is described as the fruit of the Spirit.

"But the fruit of the Spirit is love, joy, peace, forbearance, kindness, goodness, faithfulness, gentleness, and self-control." (Galatians 5:22–23a NIV)

4. <u>Spiritually</u>: When the power of the Holy Spirit is active in our lives, we become "spiritually super-charged." Each one of us has been given spiritual gifts that when driven by the Holy Spirit become extremely effective in the purposes of the Kingdom of God. This happens when we allow the Spirit to motivate us and empower us to do the things God has called us to do, and we become miraculously enabled to accomplish things far beyond our training, our skills, and even our experience.

"For in him you have been enriched in every way—with all kinds of speech and with all knowledge—Therefore you do not lack any spiritual gift." (1st Corinthians 1:5,7a NIV)

Peter was a perfect example of this. He started his journey with Jesus as an unschooled fisherman, often misunderstanding the things Jesus was talking about, and afraid to admit knowing Jesus after His arrest. However, when the Holy Spirit came upon him in Acts Chapter 2, he instantly became the most articulate and powerful speaker, preacher, and teacher of the early church. He was given incredible power to speak directly and courageously to the same people who had recently put Jesus to death, calling them murderers and charging them to repent. He was filled with wisdom, boldness, and the ability to exegete the scripture in a way that confounded the religious leaders and brought thousands of people to the Lord in one day. His spiritual gifts were ignited by the power of the Holy Spirit, and he became the most powerful apostle written about in the first half of the book of Acts.

Throughout the early church, we see common men and women operating with extraordinary power and supernatural abilities like this. Their lives were transformed from whatever they were before their spirits came alive, to what they became after their spirits were regenerated. For example, Paul began as a mean-spirited Pharisee who wanted nothing more than to chase down followers of Jesus and drag them off to jail. Even worse, he stood by and watched followers of Jesus stoned to death by angry mobs. When the power of the Holy Spirit invaded his spirit, everything changed. He became the opposite. Paul's writings contain the most tender-hearted sentiments in the New Testament. Messages like "do everything with love" and "Love is patient, love is kind" were common themes in his letters after his conversion. He spent the rest of his life traveling thousands of miles, compelling people to become followers of Jesus, and eventually was martyred for it.

This describes life in the Spirit. The Spirit empowers us with spiritual abilities that transform us from whatever we were, to powerful agents in the kingdom of God, operating with His power, for His purposes.

SPIRITUAL GIFTS, MINISTRIES, ACTIVITIES, AND MANIFESTATIONS

Paul offers a comprehensive explanation of the spiritual gifts to the Corinthian church in 1st Corinthians 12. In it we see the gifts named and listed in an organized manner:

> *Now concerning spiritual gifts, brethren, I do not want you to be ignorant: You know that you were Gentiles, carried away to these dumb idols, however, you were led. Therefore I make known to you that no one speaking by the Spirit of God calls Jesus accursed, and no one can say that Jesus is Lord except by the Holy Spirit.*

There are diversities of gifts, but the same Spirit. There are differences of ministries, but the same Lord. And there are diversities of activities, but it is the same God who works all in all. But the manifestation of the Spirit is given to each one for the profit of all:

for to one is given the word of wisdom through the Spirit,

to another the word of knowledge through the same Spirit,

to another faith by the same Spirit,

to another gifts of healings by the same Spirit,

to another the working of miracles,

to another prophecy,

to another discerning of spirits,

to another different kinds of tongues,

to another the interpretation of tongues.

But one and the same Spirit works all these things, distributing to each one individually as He wills. (1st Corinthians 12:1–11 NKJV)

Unfortunately, this section of scripture has become one of the top causes of division among churches, and denomination splits creating adversarial factions within the Body of Christ. It's sad because

Paul presents the different kinds of gifts, ministries, activities, and manifestations, as something that is meant to be beneficial for the church body, not something to divide it.

Let's look at the differences between three of the words he uses to describe the work of the Holy Spirit:

GIFTS, MINISTRIES, and ACTIVITIES:

1. <u>GIFTS</u> (Greek word: *charis*) – A gift, something *given to you, not something you acquired on your own* "Having then gifts differing according to the grace that is given to us, *let us use them*: if prophecy, *let us prophesy* in proportion to our faith; or ministry, *let us use it* in *our* ministering; he who teaches, in teaching; he who exhorts, in exhortation; he who gives, with liberality; he who leads, with diligence; he who shows mercy, with cheerfulness." (Romans 12:6–8 NKJV)

2. <u>MINISTRIES</u> (Greek word: *Diakonia*) – *The function of those who serve and equip the church* "And He Himself gave some *to be* apostles, some prophets, some evangelists, and some pastors and teachers, for the equipping of the saints for the work of *ministry*, for the edifying of the body of Christ." (Ephesians 4:11–12 NKJV)

3. <u>ACTIVITIES</u> (Greek word: *energēmatōn*) – An effect, operation, *or working of the Spirit* "And there are diversities of activities, but it is the same God who works all in all." (1st Corinthians 12:6 NKJV)

4. <u>MANIFESTATIONS</u> (Greek word: *phanerosis*) – Active exhibition of spiritual power "But the *'manifestation'* of *the Spirit* is given to each one for the profit *of all*." (1st Corinthians 12:7 NKJV)

After introducing these four areas of the works of the Holy Spirit, Paul then goes on to list what some call the "gifts" of the Holy Spirit in 1st Corinthians 12:8–10. The list, which includes nine different spiritual areas, is more specifically called a list of "manifestations of the Spirit." These manifestations are present in all the categories listed: gifts, ministries, and activities. Let's take a closer look at each of these in order to understand them better.

1. <u>Word of Wisdom</u> – Having a supernatural level of understanding over a certain situation and offering God's perspective to those who need it.

2. <u>Word of Knowledge</u> – Receiving an important piece of information from the Lord for a specific situation.

3. <u>Faith</u> – Having an extraordinarily heightened amount of trust in God's power and providence for a certain situation regardless of circumstances.

4. <u>Gifts of Healings</u> – Being used as the vessel by which God brings wellness to a person who is sick, injured, or physically, psychologically, or emotionally impaired.

5. <u>Working of Miracles</u> – Being used as the vessel by which God brings about seemingly impossible outcomes to situations in tangible and evident ways.

6. <u>Prophecy</u> – Speaking forth a message from God, which is always consistent with God's Word (not always foretelling the future).

7. <u>Discerning of Spirits</u> – Having a keen and accurate understanding of the spiritual activity that is taking place within a certain situation or with certain people.

not a special communicator *Paul*

Paul is being corrected - immature chp 10, 11

immaturity 8. <u>Different kinds of Tongues</u> – Speaking *to God* in an
unknown language. ("For he who speaks in a tongue
evangelist does not speak to men but to God." [1st Corinthians
gift 14:2a NKJV])

in languages not Babblewags

communally 9. <u>Interpretation of Tongues</u> – Being given the ability to
interpret what is being said to God by someone speaking
Acts 2 in tongues.

Being immature Many of us have discovered our spiritual gifts and have experienced what it's like to operate in these areas. It's important, however,
to not allow misunderstandings, abuses, or misuses of the spiritual
gifts and manifestations to cause us to become skeptical about them.
They are given from God for His glory, for the edification of the
church body, and even as a sign for nonbelievers. God in His sover-
eignty imparts whatever gifts He chooses to whomever He chooses.

As we continue to walk in His Spirit, God causes specific gifts
and manifestations to develop in each of us. No two people are
identical, therefore each person's giftings are uniquely different.
God has distinctly gifted each member of the Body of Christ for the
purposes of building up His church, reaching the lost, and bringing
Him glory. It's exciting to see gifts and manifestations take place as
we walk more fully in the power of the Holy Spirit, and not just in
the limited resources of the soul.

CHAPTER 8

UNITY OF THE SPIRIT

"Make every effort to keep the unity of the Spirit through the bond of peace." (Ephesians 4:3 NIV)

Before someone is made alive in the Spirit, they are incapable of relating in the realm of the spirit. Their spirit remains dead, and they are limited to interacting only in the humanity of the soul and body. Within the realm of the soul, they can communicate and in some ways even relate to those who live in the Spirit, but only as much as their thoughts and emotions will allow. We all have friends or family that we love and feel a strong connection with, maybe even have shared opinions, experiences, and even passions. Our interactions with them, however, will be devoid of any spiritual substance or resonance. This is not to say that our relationships with these people are meaningless or insignificant—they are very important—but we will not share "unity of the Spirit" with anyone until their spirits are made alive through Jesus.

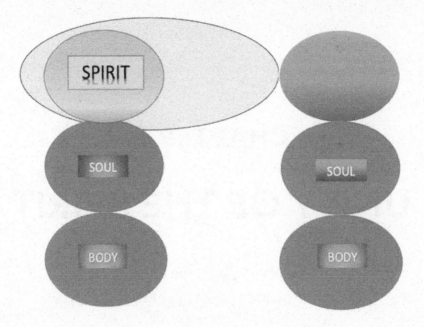

"They are darkened in their understanding and separated from the life of God because of the ignorance that is in them due to the hardening of their hearts." (Ephesians 4:18 NIV)

This scripture tells us that those who have yet to be made alive by the Spirit are separated from "the life of God" because the very means by which they can connect with God (the heart) has been hardened. This unfortunate reality is the work of the devil, which Jesus came to destroy. This is why God urges us to plead with them to be *reconciled* with Him. He wants all people to experience *abundant life* in Him.

"The thief does not come except to steal, and to kill, and to destroy. I have come that they may have *life*, and that they may have *it* more abundantly." (John 10:10 NKJV)

The abundant life God wants us to experience is unity in the Spirit with Him and each other. This is His desire for us. When two people who have been made alive in the Spirit relate to one another, something truly amazing happens. They are no longer limited to a relationship built upon common interests, mutual aspirations, shared experiences, ethnicity, culture, or even family of origin. Those who experience the unity of the Spirit are innately aware of the Holy Spirit's presence in others and in the world. They can look at one another and the world through the "eyes of the heart." They have a common view of the spiritual realities that surround them. They can share together in deep love, lasting peace, unquenchable joy, and every other benefit of the fruit of the Spirit, the power of the Spirit, and life in the Spirit. This is the essence of the word "koinonia," which is defined as a deep level of fellowship, unity, and relationship that can only take place among those who are united together in Spirit with each other, and also with Christ.

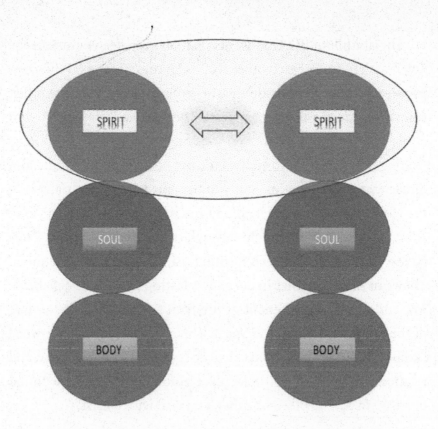

"Therefore if you have any encouragement from *being united with Christ*, if any comfort from his love, if any *common sharing in the Spirit*, if any tenderness and compassion, then make my joy complete by being like-minded, having the same love, *being one in spirit* and of one mind." (Philippians 2:1–2 NIV)

Being united with Christ means walking in His light. When we do this, two amazing things happen: we have deep fellowship with one another, and Jesus purifies us from all sin. In other words, the light of Jesus exposes, and His blood removes sin, which is the *great separator*, and the very thing that is responsible for keeping us from fellowship with God and with one another. We are able to experience deep fellowship with God and with each other. This can only take place in the light of His Spirit.

> "But if we walk in the light, as he is in the light, we have fellowship with one another, and the blood of Jesus, his Son, purifies us from all sin." (1st John 1:7 NIV)

Something that also happens, that may be more amazing than two people experiencing this type of fellowship, is when *many* people share this same level of koinonia. Jesus told us, "For where two or three gather in my name, there am I with them" (Matthew 18:20 NIV). When believers gather in His name, the Holy Spirit within them unifies them and resonates from within them creating a deep spiritual level of fellowship.

Not only can we share this level of spiritual unity with those in our church family and community but we can also find ourselves experiencing this same level of koinonia with people throughout the world whom we have never met. During my ministry travels through the years, I have had many experiences of finding instant spiritual connections and deep relationships with people whom I had just met, simply because we were united in the Spirit.

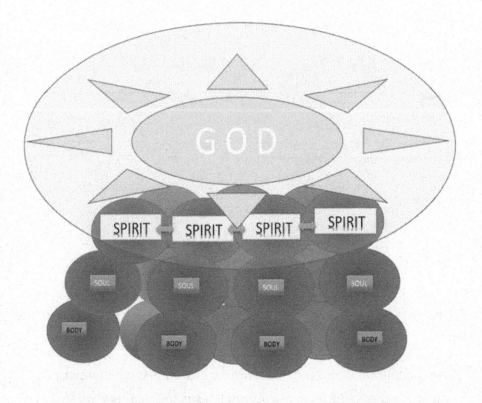

"Make every effort to keep the unity of the Spirit through the bond of peace. There is one body and one Spirit, just as you were called to one hope when you were called; one Lord, one faith, one baptism; one God and Father of all, who is over all and through all and in all." (Ephesians 4:3–6 NIV)

There is nothing sweeter and more fulfilling on earth than being part of a group of people who are truly experiencing "the unity of the Spirit and the bond of peace." We as human beings crave that type of connection. We are designed by our Creator to live in deep fellowship with one another and experience true communion with God and one another. Anything less than that is unfulfilling and never satisfying. Regardless of where we've come from ethnically, culturally, and even theologically, we are all joined together by the Spirit to be God's household. Paul compares us to a temple building, being joined together and built together as a place where God lives by His Spirit.

> "Consequently, you are no longer foreigners and strangers, but fellow citizens with God's people and also members of his household, built on the foundation of the apostles and prophets, with Christ Jesus himself as the chief cornerstone. In Him the whole building is joined together and rises to become a holy temple in the Lord. And in him, you too are being built together to become a dwelling in which God lives by his Spirit." (Ephesians 2:19–22 NIV)

In fact, it is by His Spirit that God invites us to become His children.

> ". . . you received the Spirit of adoption by whom we cry out, 'Abba, Father.' The Spirit Himself bears

witness with our spirit that we are children of God."
(Romans 8:15b–16 NKJV)

Think about the words we just read. "S*pirit of adoption*," "*cry out*," "*Abba Father*," "*our spirit*," and "*children of God*." It's fascinating that in each of these phrases we see the heart of God and His love for us displayed so clearly. Each verse reveals the method by which our heavenly Father, who longs to be reconciled with His children, brings us into complete unity with Himself through the Spirit.

Our connection with God and one another through His Spirit is what Jesus talked about with such great passion and utmost priority. When asked what the greatest commandment was, His reply was to not only love God with everything within us but also love one another. When He introduced a new commandment, it was similar. He said, "Love one another, as I have loved you." His emphasis was on bringing us into a level of unity with Himself and the Father that we could not accomplish on our own, but only through His Spirit, alive in our spirits. On His final night before the cross, he prayed for this. He asked God to bring us into the "complete unity" and love, that He and His Father experience. Pay careful attention to how He emphasizes oneness and unity. God is Spirit, so this type of unity with Him and one another cannot take place merely in the body or soul but must take place in the Spirit.

> "My prayer is not for them alone. I pray also for those
> who will believe in me through their message, that all
> of them may be *one*, Father, just as you are in me and
> I am in you. May they also be in us so that the world
> may believe that you have sent me. I have given them
> the glory that you gave me, that they may *be one as
> we are one*— I in them and you in me—so that they

may be brought to *complete unity*. Then the world will know that you sent me and have loved them even as you have loved me." (John 17:20–23 NIV).

This is the essence of *unity of the Spirit*. A unity where *His Spirit bears witness with our spirits, that we are children of God.* This is why He created us. He is a loving Father, longing for complete unity with His children, whom He loves deeply.

This cannot take place merely in the body. Our bodies are an important vessel, but they are temporary and not equipped to experience complete unity with an eternal God.

This cannot take place "solely in the soul." Our minds and emotions are extremely limited until the "eyes of our hearts" are enlightened.

This can only take place through the Spirit—His Spirit alive in our spirit. The same Spirit that hovered over the waters in the beginning and said "Let there be light!" The same Spirit that came upon young David when he was anointed by Samuel. The same Spirit that the virgin Mary encountered in Nazareth when she became the mother of our Lord. The same Spirit that Jesus promised He would send, and that the apostles experienced at Pentecost. The same Spirit that raised Jesus from the dead, and lives in us!

"If we live in the Spirit, let us also walk in the Spirit."
(Galatians 5:25 NKJV)

CHAPTER 9

CHOOSING THE SPIRIT

Examples and Practical Steps

By now you've spent a significant amount of time reading and thinking about the meanings of words like body, soul, spirit, mind, emotions, heart, and flesh. You've become acquainted with uncommon terms like tripartite and trichotomous. You've explored concepts like "believing with your heart," "living in the Spirit," and "the mind controlled by the Spirit." Now you are able to articulate those things, but you are still faced with the challenge of applying it all to your own life.

HOW DO WE CHOOSE THE SPIRIT OVER THE SOUL?

Choosing the Spirit over the soul means having our mind controlled by the Spirit instead of having it governed by the flesh. What does it look like to truly walk this out? How can we live a life that is *not* compelled "solely by the soul," but one where our soul is directed by the Holy Spirit within us so we can experience the *abundant life* and *perfect peace* that God intends for us?

Dividing the soul and the spirit is sometimes as simple as seeing the difference between man's ways or God's ways, or human knowledge versus Godly wisdom. The Word of God divides the soul and spirit by giving us examples in scripture of people who did, or did not, choose the Spirit over the soul.

Let's look at five *examples* from the Bible. Each of these people was faced with a choice of either responding out of their humanity in the soul or responding faithfully in the Spirit.

1. <u>CAESAREA PHILIPPI</u> "Never Lord!" – (*SOUL* RESPONSE)

SCENARIO: Jesus and the apostles went to the village of Caesarea Philippi. While they were there, Jesus asked the famous question, "Who do men say that I am?" Peter responded with the correct answer, "You are the Messiah, the son of the living God." Jesus, ecstatic that Peter learned this not from flesh and blood but from His Father in Heaven, began to explain to the apostles that He must die and rise again.

At that moment an exchange took place between Jesus and Peter. Jesus, operating in the Spirit, revealed His plan for death and resurrection, but Peter responded in the soul and tried to stop Him.

"From that time on Jesus began to explain to his disciples that he must go to Jerusalem and suffer many things at the hands of the elders, the chief

> priests and the teachers of the law, and that he must be killed and on the third day be raised to life.
>
> Peter took him aside and began to rebuke him. 'Never, Lord!' he said. 'This shall never happen to you!'" (Matthew 16:21–22 NIV)

SPIRIT: Jesus explained that He would go to Jerusalem to be killed, then be raised to life on the third day.

SOUL: Peter said, "Never, Lord!" "This shall never happen to you!"

Peter, operating in his mind and emotions, tried to stop Jesus from doing the most important thing that anyone had ever done in the history of the universe—the cross and the resurrection. If he had been motivated by the Spirit, he would have affirmed Jesus's plan.

2. <u>MOUNT OF TRANSFIGURATION</u> "I will put up three shelters" – (*SOUL* RESPONSE)

SCENARIO: Jesus took Peter James and John up to a high mountain and allowed them to see Him shining in the glory of God as He spoke to Moses and Elijah.

> "Peter said to Jesus, 'Lord, it is good for us to be here. If you wish, I will put up three shelters—one for you, one for Moses and one for Elijah.'While he was still speaking, a bright cloud covered them, and a voice from the cloud said, 'This is my Son, whom I love; with Him I am well pleased. Listen to him!'" (Matthew 17:4–5 NIV)

SOUL: Peter wanted to contain the glory that he was witnessing and suggested building manmade shelters.

SPIRIT: God interrupted with words of affirmation of love for His son and a command to listen to Him.

Peter once again spoke out of the impulses of his mind and emotions with an idea that was not in God's plan. The Lord quickly interrupted and quieted him.

3. HEROD KILLED JAMES "constant prayer was offered" – (*SPIRIT* RESPONSE)

SCENARIO: Severe persecution had reached the twelve apostles. Herod ordered James to be killed first. Peter was captured and would be next.

> "Peter was therefore kept in prison, but constant prayer was offered to God for him by the church." (Acts 12:5 NKJV)

SOUL: The apostles got this right. They could have easily been overcome with emotional outrage and come up with a plan to protest, revolt, or attempt to free Peter from prison. But they didn't.

SPIRIT: They prayed for him.

By the end of the chapter, not only was Peter miraculously freed from prison by an angel but Herod was also killed by an angel and eaten by worms. As a result, the Word of God continued to spread and flourish.

4. <u>PAUL PREPARES TO BE PERSECUTED</u> "compelled by the Spirit" - (*SPIRIT* RESPONSE)

SCENARIO: Paul was saying goodbye for the final time to his close friends from Ephesus. The Holy Spirit told him that he would endure harsh persecution when he left them.

"And now, compelled by the Spirit, I am going to Jerusalem, not knowing what will happen to me there. I only know that in every city the Holy Spirit warns me that prison and hardships are facing me. (Acts 20:22–23 NIV)

"When we heard this, we and the people there pleaded with Paul not to go up to Jerusalem." (Acts 21:12 NIV)

SPIRIT: Paul, compelled by the Spirit, was told to go to Jerusalem despite persecution.

SOUL: The people pleaded with Paul not to go.

Paul did not succumb to soulish dissuasion in the form of emotional pleas from his friends. He likely resisted his own rational thoughts would have kept him from imminent danger and persecution. He was told by the Holy Spirit and a prophet that he would be bound and persecuted, but he was compelled by the Spirit to go regardless. He obeyed the Holy Spirit, continued his journey, and completed the work that the Lord had for him. By the end of the book of Acts, it was said of him, "He proclaimed the kingdom of God and taught about the Lord Jesus Christ—with all boldness and without hindrance!" (Acts 28:31 NIV)

5. <u>JESUS ON THE CROSS</u> "Father forgive them" – (*JESUS'S* RESPONSE)

SCENARIO: Jesus had just endured extreme torture and humiliation at the hands of the Romans. His back was severely lacerated from the ruthless whipping. His head was bleeding profusely from the crown of thorns. His body was so physically spent from the blood loss, battering, and dehydration that he could not carry his cross for the full duration of the journey up to Golgotha, where he would be crucified.

> "When they came to the place called the Skull, they crucified him there, along with the criminals—one on his right, the other on his left. Jesus said, 'Father, forgive them, for they do not know what they are doing.'" (Luke 23:33–34a NIV)

SOUL: The natural response from the soul and the body would have reasonably been a reaction of outrage, self-preservation, and wrath. A violent and vengeful retaliation to the extreme pain that was being inflicted upon Him would have been expected and justified.

SPIRIT: Jesus, who always acted and spoke from the Spirit, responded in this way, "Father, forgive them, for they do not know what they are doing."

His willingness to forgive those who were crucifying Him was not a physical, mental, or emotional reaction, it was a response from His Spirit. Sometimes the most spiritual thing we can do is forgive, especially when everything in our soul compels us not to.

Jesus's life gave us many perfect examples of what it looks like to choose the Spirit over the soul. He never allowed His mind or emotions to direct His will contrary to the will of God. Although He was fully divine, He was also fully human and faced many of the same struggles and challenges that we do.

We see from the gospels that He experienced many deep emotions and strong feelings throughout His life on earth. He cried when His friend Lazarus died (John 11:35). He wept over Jerusalem when they rejected Him (Luke 19:41). He even sweat droplets of blood due to the tremendous agony He was feeling in the garden of Gethsemane on the night before His crucifixion (Luke 22:44). On that particular night, Jesus gave us a glimpse into *His own soul.* **Yes, Jesus was both fully God and fully human, with a human soul just like us.**

> "He said to them, '*My soul* is overwhelmed with sorrow to the point of death. Stay here and keep watch with me.'" (Matthew 26:38 NIV)

It was then that He uttered His famous words that proved to us that *even He* needed to surrender His will, to the will of the Father,

> "Father, if you are willing, take this cup from me; yet not my will, but yours be done" (Luke 22:42 NIV).

Jesus knew that doing the Father's will was the very reason He came to earth. He would let nothing stand in the way.

"For I have come down from heaven not to do *my will* but to do the will of him who sent me." (John 6:38 NIV)

Although He was passionate and sensitive and had very strong feelings, He was fully surrendered to the will of the Father in everything that He said and did. He never allowed His feelings, emotions, or even His own will to take precedence over God's will for His life.

This is what it means to choose the Spirit over the soul.

It means choosing to allow His Word to govern our thoughts.

It means choosing to allow His Spirit to control our emotions.

It means choosing His will to prevail over our will.

PRACTICAL STEPS

BE WILLING

You must be willing to be led by the Spirit and to trust in His Word.

You must be willing to relinquish your own, thoughts, feelings, and ideas as the basis for your opinions, attitudes, and actions. The Lord will not violate your will and intrude upon your unwillingness. This may require you to invite Him to restore you and ask Him to give you a willing spirit. This is what David prayed when he realized that his choices and transgressions had brought him far from the will of God.

"Restore to me the joy of your salvation, and grant me a *willing spirit.*" (Psalm 51:12a NIV)

If you cling to your own will and are reluctant to surrender to God's Word, you will never experience the life and peace that He intends for you. You will be vulnerable to a life of worry, anger, and unfulfillment. You must remain receptive to the Holy Spirit's leading and also be willing to do what is needed to please Him.

"Whoever sows to please their flesh, from the flesh will reap destruction; whoever sows to please the Spirit, from the Spirit will reap eternal life." (Galatians 6:8 NIV)

TRUST THE WORD OF GOD

If you doubt the Word of God, ignore it, or if you simply don't know it, you will not be able to fully implement the wisdom, guidance, and instruction from the Word of God, especially where it specifically instructs us to walk, live, and operate in the Spirit.

We also must recognize the importance and role of the Word of God in our key verse:

"For the word of God is alive and active. Sharper than any double-edged sword, it penetrates even to dividing soul and spirit." (Hebrews 4:12a NIV)

The Word of God is the *divider* between the soul and the spirit. It helps us determine the difference between a soul reaction and the Spirit's leading. We need to rely on God's Word to help us figure out if we are reacting in the soul, or truly being led by God's Spirit within us. We must trust that His word is applicable to every situation we face.

The author of Hebrews tells us that the Word of God is "living and active," which means that is not relegated to just printed words on a page or text on a screen. It is alive and available to us in real time, applying to every situation and circumstance we experience, as we are experiencing them.

WELCOME THE HOLY SPIRIT

The Word of God *becomes* "living and active" when we *invite* the Holy Spirit to help us understand it. As we read God's Word, the Holy Spirit highlights things and helps us understand the truth of His Word. Jesus tells us that the Holy Spirit not only *teaches us* but also *reminds us* of His Words.

> "But the Advocate, the Holy Spirit, whom the Father will send in my name, will teach you all things and will remind you of everything I have said to you." (John 14:26 NIV)

We must rely upon the Holy Spirit to be our trusted helper and our guide. It can be tricky to navigate the inclinations of the soul without the Holy Spirit's guidance. If we *operate* and *make decisions* only from our minds and emotions, without being guided and directed by the Holy Spirit, we can easily lose sight of God's truth. The Holy Spirit is the one who guides us into all truth. We cannot find truth if we rely only upon the resources of the soul.

> "But when He, the Spirit of truth, comes, He will guide you into all the truth." (John 16:13a NIV)

TAKE EVERY THOUGHT CAPTIVE

Many of us have seen the popular diagrams used in psychology to describe how our thoughts lead to behaviors. The idea is that *thoughts* lead to *feelings*, which develop into *emotions* that can lead to *actions* or *behavior*. A *thought*, if left to linger or wander in our mind, can lead to *feelings* and *emotions* that we will usually *act* upon. We must be proactive with our thoughts. Our minds and thoughts are not uncontrollable. Our thoughts must be taken captive and made subject to the Word of God and obedient to Christ.

> ". . . take captive every thought to make it obedient to Christ." (2nd Corinthians 10:5b NIV)

This may seem impossible to you, but it's not. The lies of the deceiver will tell you that you are a slave to your mind and a prisoner of your emotions. You are tempted to believe that you have no choice but to be subject to the whims of your thoughts and feelings, but this is precisely the lie that the enemy uses to keep you walking in the flesh instead of living in the Spirit. The Holy Spirit will help you with this also.

When negative, deceptive, or even evil thoughts enter your mind, the Holy Spirit can give you the power to overcome them. Paul tells Timothy that fear and timidity are not from the Holy Spirit, but power, love, and a sound mind are given to us by Him.

> "For God has not given us a spirit of fear, but of power and of love and of a sound mind." (2nd Timothy 1:7 NKJV)

With the self-discipline of a sound mind, we have the ability to direct our minds toward the things that are true, right, and even lovely.

> "Finally, brothers and sisters, whatever is true, whatever is noble, whatever is right, whatever is pure, whatever is lovely, whatever is admirable—if anything is excellent or praiseworthy—think about such things." (Philippians 4:8 NIV)

AVOID THE PATTERN OF THE WORLD

"Do not conform to the pattern of this world." (Romans 12:2a NIV)

Lately, the "pattern of this world" seem to be characterized by *fear* and *anxiety*, which lead to *anger* and *outrage*. Fear and anger are being normalized in our society. Society has become fixated on fear and people have become addicted to outrage. The news and social media try to keep us in continual crisis mode with a constant barrage of disturbing headlines, incendiary comments, and a ceaseless offering of clickbait.

Recently a director from a major news network was quoted as saying, "Fear sells," referring to an industry tactic known as fear-based marketing, which is, in essence, a form of fearmongering. Media outlets know that promoting *fear* and *anger* is beneficial to ratings and viewership, which translates to influence and profitability.

Unquestionably, there are many terrible things going on in our world every day. This has always been the case, and no generation was ever without its share of horrific catastrophes, natural disasters, awful injustices, and global crises. King Solomon once said:

> "What has been will be again, what has been done will be done again; there is nothing new under the sun." (Ecclesiastes 1:9 NIV)

This verse underscores the fact that there has always been trouble in the world and there will always be trouble in the world. Jesus mentions it as well, and also tells us how we should react to it:

> "These things I have spoken to you, that in Me you may have peace. In the world you will have tribulation, but be of good cheer, I have overcome the world." (John 16:33 NKJV)

While trouble and tribulation have always existed in our world, it's only been in recent history that people have had continual, uninterrupted access to information about it. In the modern age, information is accessible in real time. Troubling stories and images are constantly at our fingertips and on screens all around us.

Our soulish response to upsetting information is typically feelings of *fear, helplessness, anxiety, uncertainty, anger,* and *outrage.* Our spiritual response to this type of bad news is *faith, hope, trust,* and *peace* when we choose to walk in the Spirit.

We must remember that *nothing happens unless God lets it happen, or makes it happen.* He is never caught by surprise, and He is never defeated or overcome by evil. We have to trust Him. The next time you are given the opportunity to fear, don't take it. Instead, be of good cheer and rest in the fact that although you may not fully understand it, He has overcome the world. Shield your mind from the influences of fear, anger, and the evil of this world. Protect yourself from the contagious poison in the deceptive messages all around you. Protect your peace, and the peace of your household, and above all else, guard your heart.

> "Above all else, guard your heart, for everything you
> do flows from it." (Proverb 4:23 NIV)

HAVE YOUR MIND RENEWED

Many of us come to God with minds that are in desperate need of renewal. It's easy over time to develop habits and patterns that respond negatively to the things of God. Maybe you've developed attitudes and a temperament that are inclined to defy or reject the prompting of the Holy Spirit.

This is usually a result of living apart from God's will and hardening our hearts to the voice of the Holy Spirit. It can also be a symptom of having a wounded soul. The pattern of the world is characterized by sin. The results of sin, whether committed by us or committed against us, have a detrimental effect on our souls. Our minds become darkened and our emotions become calloused in an attempt to cover our shame or defend against the hurt we feel. This pattern drives us away from the plan that God has for our souls. It causes us to act, speak, and behave out of bitterness, anger, and fear instead of God's good, pleasing, and perfect will.

> "They are darkened in their understanding and
> separated from the life of God because of the
> ignorance that is in them due to the hardening of
> their hearts."(Ephesians 4:18 NIV)

The first step toward the renewing of our minds is asking the Lord for healing so that the wounds of the past will no longer have a grip on us. We may need to ask God for forgiveness for things that we've held onto that have become toxic to our souls. It may also require offering forgiveness to those we hold bitterness toward so that we can be free from the effects of whatever was done to us. We may need transformation from what we are now to what God wants us to be in our minds and the emotions of our very souls. This type of transformation can only come through the renewal of our minds.

". . . be transformed by the renewing of your mind. Then you will be able to test and approve what God's will is—his good, pleasing and perfect will." (Romans 12:2b NIV)

CREATE A LIFESTYLE OF PRAYER

It would be difficult to be led by the Spirit without adequate communication with God. Because of what Jesus did by reconciling us with the Father, we can experience God's presence whenever we want. God wants us to come and talk to Him. Prayer is an expression of our being that is inherently spiritual.

We must prioritize and maintain our prayer life by committing to a lifestyle of prayer every day. Spending time with God allows the Holy Spirit to help us navigate through the thoughts and feelings of our soul in order to lead us to His truth. God wants us to know Him and also be known by Him.

If we commit to spending time with God regularly, we will find that our spirit becomes stronger and our soul becomes more aware of the reality of the Spirit. If we neglect a lifestyle of prayer, we remain limited to the mundane realm of thoughts and feelings. As we spend time with God, we will find ourselves worrying less and worshipping more. Worry will give way to assurance and trust, and worship will bring us into more of an awareness of His presence. As a result, we will experience His peace, His perfect peace that passes all understanding. Once you've experienced this, you will realize that His peace is the very thing that your soul craves and was designed to experience. You'll be overcome with such a sense of completeness and wholeness in your body, soul, and spirit that you will no longer be subject to the volatility of your thoughts and feelings, or the instability of your mind and emotions.

As your focus shifts from soul to Spirit, you will find that you will worry less and pray more. You'll freely make your needs known to God and thank Him for all He has done for you. Then you will experience the most amazing part of the journey: *peace*! Not just temporary peace in the absence of chaos, but His peace that surpasses all human understanding.

> "Don't worry about anything; instead, *pray about everything*. Tell God what you need, and thank him for all he has done. Then you will experience God's *peace*, which exceeds anything we can understand. *His peace* will guard your hearts and minds as you live in Christ Jesus." (Philippians 4:6–7 NLT)

This peace is given to us by the "God of peace."

It's a peace that the world can't offer.

It's the peace of Jesus, the Prince of Peace.

It's the peace that can fill every part of your tripart being—your whole *spirit, soul,* and *body.*

"May God himself, the *God of peace*, sanctify you through and through. May your whole *spirit, soul* and *body* be kept blameless at the coming of our Lord Jesus Christ." (1st Thessalonians 5:23 NIV)

NOTES

1. A. B. Simpson – *Wholly Sanctified*

2. Chuck Smith: *Verse by Verse Study on Galatians*

3. C. H. Spurgeon – *The Soul Winner*

4. Watchman Nee – *The Spiritual Man*

5. A. W. Tozer – *Recognizing the Witness of the Spirit – The Alliance Tozer Devotional*

6. Dr. Ben Carson – *Under Our Skin* – Benjamin Watson (pg. 191)

7. Dr. Martin Luther King Jr. – *The Essential Martin Luther King Jr.*

8. Watchman Nee – *The Spiritual Man*

9. Chuck Smith – *Verse by Verse Study on Galatians*

10. A. W. Tozer – *We Travel an Appointed Way*

11. C. H. Spurgeon – *The Soul Winner*

ABOUT THE AUTHOR

RAPHAEL GIGLIO is the Founding and Lead Pastor of North Shore Fellowship in New Jersey and is ordained by The Christian and Missionary Alliance. He is a graduate of Pillar College with a degree in organizational leadership and has studied religion and journalism at Harvard and Rutgers Universities.

Raised in New Jersey, Raphael is the youngest of six sons in an Italian/Jewish family of twelve children. At age ten, Raphael was introduced to faith in Jesus as Messiah by his Jewish grandfather during the Jesus Movement of the early 70's.

As a teenager, he attended the discipleship training schools of both YWAM and Last Days Ministries in Lindale, Texas.

As a young adult, Raphael signed his first recording contract with the Christian music label Myrrh Records in Nashville, TN, and worked as a professional musician. After a career in songwriting, recording, and touring, he went on to become a manager for Capitol Records Nashville, working in various positions within the music industry.

Raphael's passion for teaching the Word of God led him to transition his focus to Christian ministry and church planting. He was eventually ordained as a pastor at New River Fellowship in

Franklin, TN where he served for many years before being called back to the Northeast.

Raphael has been serving as a pastor for over twenty years and has a strong desire to help people understand the importance of the Word of God, life in the Spirit, and the Hebrew roots of Christianity.

Raphael and his wife Aly currently live at the New Jersey Shore with their twin daughters Abigail and Phoebe.